The Magical Notary Art

Sigils, Seals, Notaries & Signatures

ABOUT THE AUTHOR

Frater Barrabbas Tiresius is a practicing ritual magician who has studied magic and the occult for over forty years. He believes that ritual magic is a discipline whose mystery is unlocked by continual practice and by occult experiences and revelations. Frater Barrabbas believes that traditional approaches should be balanced with creativity and experimentation and that no occult or magical tradition is exempt from changes and revisions.

Frater Barrabbas also founded a magical order called the Order of the Gnostic Star and is an elder and lineage holder in the Alexandrian tradition of Witchcraft.

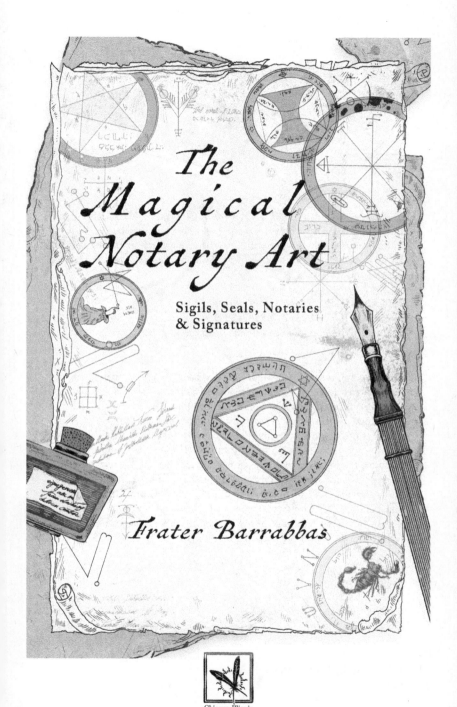

The Magical Notary Art: Sigils, Seals, Notaries & Signatures © 2025 by Frater Barrabbas. All rights reserved. No part of this book may be reproduced in any manner whatsoever without written permission from Crossed Crow Books, except in the case of brief quotations embodied in critical articles and reviews.

Paperback ISBN: 978-1-959883-96-8
Hardcover ISBN: 978-1-964537-39-9
Library of Congress Control Number on file.

Disclaimer: Crossed Crow Books, LLC does not participate in, endorse, or have any authority or responsibility concerning private business transactions between our authors and the public. Any internet references contained in this work were found to be valid during the time of publication, however, the publisher cannot guarantee that a specific reference will continue to be maintained. This book's material is not intended to diagnose, treat, cure, or prevent any disease, disorder, ailment, or any physical or psychological condition. The author, publisher, and its associates shall not be held liable for the reader's choices when approaching this book's material. The views and opinions expressed within this book are those of the author alone and do not necessarily reflect the views and opinions of the publisher.

Published by:
Crossed Crow Books, LLC
6934 N Glenwood Ave, Suite C
Chicago, IL 60626
www.crossedcrowbooks.com

Printed in the United States of America.
IBI

Dedication

This book is dedicated to Blake Malliway, who requested that I write it and who inspired me to develop it; to Sara Mastros, a newly made friend and brilliant magician; to my wife Joni, who taught me how to write books; to Lynxa, my feline muse; and to the many Witches, ritual magicians, and occultists who will find this book useful and helpful in developing their magical rites.

Acknowledgements

Many thanks to Crossed Crow Books, whose artistry, editing acumen, and support made this book project possible. And to Wycke Malliway, whose creativity always helps to make my book projects graphically and esthetically pleasing.

CONTENTS

The Unexpected Book Project: Note by Frater Barrabbas..... xi
Foreword................................... xvi

Introduction to the Magical Notary Art • 1

Modern Sigil Magic and Words of Power 3
Notary Art of Magic 6
Information Model and Information Theory 7
A Book on Sigil Magic: The Notary Art 10

Part I
Sigils, Seals, and Signatures for Spirits

Chapter One
Brief Discussion About Planetary Kameas and Magic Squares • 16

List of Magical Squares and their Attributions.... 19

Chapter Two
Alphabet Wheels: Hebrew, Greek, and Latin • 27

Constructing Sigils Using Alphabet Wheels 31
Drawing and Making Spirit Sigils.............. 33

Chapter Three
Brief Discussion About Angelic and Demonic Seals • 38

Demonic Seals. 39
Angelic Seals. 45
Constructing Magical Seals. 49

Chapter Four
Condensing Letter Forms into Magical Signatures • 53

Constructing a Spirit's Mark or Magical Signature . 54
Using the Tarot to Define a Spirit's Qualities 56

Part II
Alphabet of Aspirations: Sigils, Words, and Phrases of Power

Chapter Five
Method of Sigil Creation from Words and Phrases • 65

Power of Pictograms 71
Words of Power, Chants, and Mantras. 73
Spare's Alphabet of Desire: A Brief Overview 75

Chapter Six
Magical Alphabets: A Brief Overview • 79

Magical Formulas and Letter to
Number Translations. 82

Chapter Seven
Magical Notaries: A Brief Overview • 89

Part III
Rites of Sigil, Seal, Notae, and Signature Consecration

Chapter Eight
Consecrating and Charging Sigils, Seals, and Notae • 99

Use of Sacraments for Consecration 100
Methods of Charging and Consecration 103
Triple Consecration for Spirit or
Godhead Placeholders...................... 106

Part IV
Magical Uses of Sigils, Seals, Notae, and Signatures

Chapter Nine
Foundational Rites Used in the Notary Art • 111

Meditation is the Key to the Notary Art 112
Divination and Sacred Space.................. 115
Energy Model Magical Operations 117
Spirit Model Magical Operations 123
Preparation Steps 129
Conjuration Rite........................... 130
Psychological and Temporal Model
Magical Operations........................ 134

Chapter Ten
Using the Notary Art in Magical Rites • 138

Imprinting and Directing Raised Energy Fields .. 140
Symbolic Naming for Invoked or Evoked Spirits.. 142

Building a Temporal Link and
Directing Talismans. 144
Deity Placeholders and Naming
Animated Statues or Pictures. 146
Information Magical Model: Using
Consecrated Sigils and Notae Alone 148

Conclusion
Pulling It All Together: Language and the Notary Art of Magic • 153

Bibliography *157*
Index. *159*

THE UNEXPECTED BOOK PROJECT: NOTE BY FRATER BARRABBAS

I WAS SITTING AT A TABLE going over some book project notes at Convocation 2024 after the convention ended when I got some text messages from Blake, my publisher. I had missed him and his team when they had departed, and he sent a few messages while he was driving back to Chicago from Ann Arbor. He asked me if I would consider writing a book on sigil magic. I hadn't considered writing such a book, and I told him so, but after thinking about it for a short time, I decided to reply in the affirmative. This book was unplanned by me, but for some reason as I sat there working over a potential table of contents, the book came together in my mind as a complete and comprehensive package. I was surprised, but I have been using sigils, seals, and even notae for many years, so pulling together how I would approach a book on this topic turned out to be quite easy.

Now I wasn't going to start writing another book until later this autumn, but this project was given to me by my publishers, and I was able to envision it without any effort. So, here we are, expounding on a topic that I hadn't anticipated writing about and engaging with a book-writing project well before I expected to. We could call this book "the unexpected book project" as sort of a joke on "the unexpected party" in the fictional work by Tolkien, *The Hobbit*. My magical process had suddenly become more mysterious to me. Some events can turn out quite unexpectedly in the life of a Witch, ritual magician, teacher, and author.

When I got home from the convention, I put my thoughts and ideas to paper, produced a table of contents, and wrote up the first chapter. I verified that there was indeed a good market niche for this book and sent my proposal to Crossed Crow Books. They liked what they saw and sent me a contract. While organizing my ideas, I was inspired by a term that I had encountered in my studies of medieval magic that classified various symbols, seals, sigils, spirit names, and occult graphic representations as being part of a notary art of magic, and I decided to use that term to classify this work.

Whatever methodology you might use to capture the name and essence of a spirit in a two-dimensional form or to encapsulate an objective or aspiration, such as a sigil, seal, signature, or mark, the mechanism used would have been called the "notary art" in the late Middle Ages. There is the obvious but obscure grimoire called *Ars Notoria of Solomon,* which combines divinely inspired geometric designs with prayers, the garbled names of angels, and words of power. The later use of sigils was derived from magical squares, angelic and Goetic demon seals and, even later, Austin Spare's system of sigil magic and magical graphic design. All three of these approaches share a common thread: they are represented by a system of writing, symbols, and graphical representations that use words and symbolic images to encapsulate and communicate identities, ideas, and expressions in a purely magical manner. It is an art of creating magical forms and ideograms that represent the expression of magic itself.

A notary, from ancient times, was a secretary who wrote in shorthand and kept written records, reports, and contractual agreements. He was typically an individual who knew legal matters and could represent various parties or function as a witness to agreements and contracts. In a completely magical and occult context, the notary becomes the magician who scribed agreements between spiritual parties and who used the art of magical words, signs, and symbols to generate magical effects for themselves or paying clients. All of these literary and graphic arts can be grouped under the topic of the "magical notary art," so I have decided to call this book, which will examine these methodologies and techniques, the same. I believe that this archaic term perfectly represents this entire class of magical work, and that it can be dusted off and used in a post-modern context as any kind of literary or graphical magical work.

Based on this understanding of the notary art, I have included all of the arts that I have practiced—and a few that I haven't—into a single concise book that examines the full spectrum of practices and techniques associated with this work. There isn't a book that contains all of these techniques together, and while this will not be an exhaustive work (since that would make it far too large to be practical), it will still be an important compendium of the notary art. Using the Goldilocks approach to writing, it will not be too small nor too large, but instead, just right.

The notary art of magic produces a quantifiable product, which is a sigil, seal, signature, or nota with a magical quality by itself. This art literally makes magic. However, that magic is always latent until it is properly consecrated and charged. Some will disagree with this statement, but the employment of a sigil or seal is a deliberative task, so consecration and charging would represent the final step in activating such a tool.

However, I should note that a well-developed and artistically rendered magical graphic representation does have an impact on the mind of the magician and others who might be exposed to it. The imagination is a powerful tool that the ritual magician employs with a certain artistic genius, but I still hold that a magical artifact, such as a sigil or seal, is activated through the art of consecration. It might beguile the eyes and the senses, but that is the latent potential associated with a good graphic design. Potentials can also have effects, so engage in caution while experimenting with the notary art, since even a latent artifact can have an effect, including an unwanted one.

So, you have been warned about the potential problems that making a magical graphic design might produce. My approach is to always create the sigil or seal and then consecrate it soon after. I like to take such tools and sequester them until they are to be used in a ritual working. Still, an unconsecrated sigil or seal must also be sequestered until the ritual magician employs it, just to be safe and smart in its use.

Since the notary art is a magical art form, it is important to practice it often and develop graphic skills over time. An important concept is esthetics, and the better artistic outcome will produce a more powerful artifact. Learning to design, plan, draw, and execute a magical graphic design is an important skill, and one that needs to be developed and mastered after much practice. Experimentation and consistency are also important, and collecting drafting tools; pens, pencils, ink, and paint; and parchment, tag board, plywood, or metallic badges is the key to producing optimal examples of the notary art. I have often enjoyed manufacturing magical tools using this artform, and I believe that you will find it fun and extremely useful too.

Smoking a bowl with Frater B.

FOREWORD

I have never smoked pipeweed with Gandalf, but I imagine I am not the only magician who longs to. The experience of reading *The Magical Notary Art* is a lot like I imagine that would be. Frater Barrabbas Tiresius has been doing important work in both Witchcraft and ritual magic for almost as long as I've known how to read, and this book is an invitation to sit at the fire with an affable elder and shoot the shit about magic.

In this book, Frater Barrabbas revives the term "notary art" for the vast category of written and drawn magic. In a direct and conversational tone, he gives a fun overview of a variety of basic building blocks of notary magic, including sigils, seals, signs, symbols, and ciphers. At every step, Frater Barrabbas encourages the reader to experiment and build their own practices. Unlike many other texts on the topic, this one focuses on an informational model of magic and avoids getting too bogged down in hermetic foofaraw. The focus on general theory over specific techniques allows for easy "plug and play" adaptability to many styles of magic.

In addition to history and theory, Frater Barrabbas provides detailed step-by-step instructions for creating and deploying many kinds of notary magic. And yet, this book isn't just a compilation of techniques: it provides a coherent "big picture" view of the nature of magical symbolism as well as its practical application, all arranged to gently guide the learner from basic to more sophisticated practices. Throughout, Frater Barrabbas emphasizes the importance of practice and experimentation, offering encouragement and inspiration to both beginners and more intermediate practitioners.

Of particular value is Chapter Seven, on the 13th century Latin grimoire (wizard textbook) after which this text is named. *The Ars Notoria* ("The Notary Art") was intended primarily for those training for clerical careers as priests, scribes, and other literate professionals. It promised them forbidden sorcerous methods to work with angels and other spirits to learn rapidly and easily—a sort of magical Adderall.

The root of the word *notoria* is "notae." As you can probably tell, the word notae is the root of the English word "note." It is a Latin word indicating all sorts of writing, diagrams, and illustrations. In the *Ars Notoria*, the word notae is a technical term used for a particular type of mystical diagram. These gorgeous medieval illuminations are replete with angel figures, magic words, and mysterious cosmic cartography. If you grew up in Christendom, when you try to imagine a badass diagram from a medieval wizard textbook, you're probably imagining something very close to the notae of *Ars Notoria*. In addition to being illustrative diagrams, these notae are also objects of ritual contemplation, worked in concert with a system of magical orations. With this practice, the reader is promised, one can dramatically improve their ability to learn. I made extensive use of this text in graduate school and highly recommend it to other magic-minded nerds.

After introducing *Ars Notoria*, Frater Barrabbas offers a brief (but tantalizing) discussion about the differences between learning in the 13th century and today. In that context, he then offers a new interpretation of the concept of notae designed for the same purpose: to open the mental gates of learning and creativity. As an author most well-known for my fussy translations of fussy historic magic, some might expect me to look down my nose at this kind of modern eclecticism. But, as in the Latin *Ars Notoria*, there is a method to the madness!

The Latin *Ars Notoria* teaches the art of learning as applied to clerical studies in the 13th century. That art was primarily about the rote memorization of large, human-manageable amounts of data. Today, however, our primary challenge as twenty-first-century learners is different. We swim in almost unfathomable amounts of data; our challenge is to navigate it with discernment, creativity, and wisdom. The flexibility of mind which Fr. Barrabas demonstrates with this free-wheeling syncretism is the exact notary art that helps a human outhink even the best thinking machine. This is particularly evident in the example notae given at the end of the chapter. In my opinion, Chapter Seven is the real gem of this book (and well worth the price of purchase). This book provides a truly cosmopolitan practice, examining magic from many different cultures and combining them into simple practices for beginner magicians eager to learn.

— Sara Mastros, author of *Introduction to Witchcraft* and *The Sorcery of Solomon*

INTRODUCTION TO THE MAGICAL NOTARY ART

SIGILS AND SEALS HAVE BEEN THE FOCUS of the practice of magical invocation and evocation since antiquity. It is an art form that seeks to determine the mark, pictogram, or symbolic signature that encapsulates and identifies the spirit within the domain of Spirit. It is an artistic rendering of a custom symbol that acts as a key to the identity of a spirit that can be used in this world and the other worlds where spirits reside. It can also be a symbolic graphic expression for a desire or aspiration, or a doorway into another world. It is, in fact, any kind of graphic representation of a magical artifact, whether produced by words, phrases, images, numbers, or any combination.

The word "sigil" comes from the Latin word *sigillum*, which means "seal," represented by the lozenge of wax that was imprinted by a stamp or engraved ring to close or seal a letter or legitimize a legal document like a signature. A similar term to the word sigil is the Hebrew word *segulah*, which means "treasure" akin to "magical virtue." In the context of a magical working, the word or action represents a ritual action or the utterance of a magical word of power. What this means is that a sigil can denote a number of different kinds of tools or artifacts. A sigil representing the name of spirit is written on a piece of parchment and then, through the artifice of ritual, consecrated or made holy.

A magician who possesses a consecrated and charged sigil or seal in addition to the specific name of a spirit has everything required to summon or call that spirit from its domain into ours. In fact, there seems to be an almost legal quality to using a consecrated sigil or seal, where it functions as a kind of spiritual subpoena ordering an entity to come before the "court" of the magician. In fact, if you consider that an evocation also includes a legally binding agreement (pact) between the magician and the spirit, and that the seal is that entity's mark or signature associated with that agreement, then what we are describing is a quasi-legal proceeding functioning within the occult activity of summoning a spirit. While the legalities might be theologically questionable to orthodox religious thought, the medieval legal mind intrinsically entertains this kind of approach to magic, which likely had its origin in the late Roman empire, where such legalities reached their apex of use.

The notary art is also a part of this magical and spiritual process, although as represented in the medieval work *Ars Notoria of Solomon*, it does not engage in evocation, nor does it seek to materialize spirits in this world. However, as depicted in the grimoire, it uses a combination of symbolic artistic designs (notae) with prayers incorporating angel names of unknown origin to elevate the operator to the spiritual realm. The word *nota*, which means "a mark" in Latin, combined with the concept of a *notary*, or a legal witness to a contract, extends the concept of a sigil or seal used to conjure a spirit and a pact that establishes a binding agreement. Notary art is elevated to a spiritual exercise, it uses symbolic structures and words of power to weave a magic spell to open the operator to the spiritual domain. Notary art is then the blending of symbols and words of power (names of angels, Deity, or phrases from holy scripture) to produce magical devices that can function as a gateway between the worlds of matter, mind, and spirit. We can see many examples of this art, including the planetary pentacles in the *Key of Solomon*.

Sigils as linear representations of a spirit's name are to be found in literature, particularly in the second book of Agrippa's *Occult Philosophy*, where they are briefly shown as the product of tracing the names of the angelic spirits associated with the planets to the planetary tables.

The tables or magical squares are also used to trace out the magical seals for each of the planets, representing an artful method of linearly connecting all of the cells in the table. This methodology enables the magician to produce sigils for the planetary ruling angels for a given planet, but correspondingly, cannot be used to fashion sigils for spirits who do not fit into one of the seven planetary tables, although they could be attributed in some manner as long as the spirit's name can be written in Hebrew letters. These magic squares are an independent magical artform, and they are also called the *Kameas*, and the planetary seals and sigils are derived from them.

Magical squares are a complete and separate discipline of magic, and they can be found in many sources, from Hebrew, Latin, or Greek alphabets to pure numbers. While sigils and seals were originally derived from magical squares, they wield a powerful magic by themselves. This is quite obvious when one considers that the *Book of Abramelin the Sage* has such a high degree of fame and infamy based almost solely on the large collection of magical squares found within its pages.

MODERN SIGIL MAGIC AND WORDS OF POWER

Modern adaptations to the art of sigil magic gave it a greater utility. The Golden Dawn used an alphabet wheel consisting of three concentric circles to represent the three groupings of the Hebrew letters and placed it in the center of their Rose Cross artifact. Using this wheel allows the operator to fashion a linear sigil for any spirit name that can be spelled using Hebrew letters. Based on various ideas and suggestions, I have come up with alphabet wheels for Greek and Latin letters that can be used along with the Hebrew wheel to derive a sigil for any spirit name in the Western Mystery Tradition. I have found that using alphabet wheels gives the operator greater flexibility and allows for a more concise and direct mechanism for determining a sigil. There is no need to substitute letters for numbers, and you can more easily visualize the sigil as you are drawing it on the wheel. You can find an example of using an alphabet wheel drawing the sigil for the spirit Vasago in Chapter Two, page 35.

Another more modern approach—and one which has probably the most amazing technique for producing sigils—is the method that was developed by Austin Spare. Spare sought to produce sigils from words and phrases and develop a kind of hieroglyphic and pictogram representation for aspirations and desires. While his method could also produce sigils for the names of spirits, it was typically used to produce magical hieroglyphics to encapsulate and symbolize a magical objective. It is a process of reducing the forms and structures of letters to their most basic occurrences and then artfully reassembling them to form a symbolic structure that fully represents that word or phrase in the spirit world. Spare's sigil magic, a method of graphically symbolizing desires and aspirations, is a complete magical discipline by itself, although it can be used along with energy-based magical operations to forge a magical link and imprint that sigil upon a raised energy field, giving it a target and direction.

Sigils of aspiration, as Spare's system is called, are different than name sigils in that they are symbolized graphic representations of magical objectives. Where sigil names communicate directly with the spirit world to contact and constrain a spirit in the evocation process, a sigil of aspiration is a symbolic graphic structure that communicates an objective, which impacts both the domain of spirit and the collective consciousness of the culture, and rebounds or echoes back to the material plane to bend probabilities so that the aspiration might be fully realized. There is no spiritual intermediary in this kind of magic, but there is a binding relationship between these worlds of spirit, mind, and matter, so that what is symbolically communicated in one will powerfully affect the others.

There is also a history of using magical alphabets to disguise a name or a word and give it significance in the spirit world. These magical alphabets are a part of the magical traditions of the medieval and Renaissance periods, but they may have a deeper historical significance. If we consider that reading and writing were once considered magical operations only a few centuries ago, the magic of letters and words, whatever language they would have been written in, would have been considered magical ideograms by themselves, particularly if they spelled out sacred names, quotations from scripture, or unknown words of power.

This approach of using magical alphabets in magic thus has an ancient provenance. Part of the power of the Enochian language developed by Dee and Kelly is the magical alphabet used to write that language on the various Enochian tools and artifacts. If we also include the use of ciphers and cryptograms to disguise writings, particularly if they are occult or magical texts, then we have another kind of magical translation process that gives the notary art its particular power and mystery. We can also see this in the production of magical talismans that use words and phrases as well as the use of phylacteries, writings on cloth or leather, or the wearing of religiously significant texts folded into small containers and worn or tied onto the body of the magician to assist in empowering them with the noumena of sacred words or phrases.

It would seem that the magical power of words and geometric and iconic symbols have a particular, important place in the practice of magic. We can see this as a metaphysical principle for the use of language in the occult arts. According to Agrippa, language represents the highest of the three methods or traditions of magic and is the essence of Qabalistic magic. The Egyptian tradition of magic relied on barbarous words of evocation that are so powerful that, even today, we can sense the force of these exhortations when they are used in a modern magical context. Part of the appeal of the *Greek Magical Papyri* (*PGM*) are the words of power found in the various incantations, which are also still highly potent to this day. The *PGM* also has geometric ideograms and magical markings to accompany the words of powers, along with material fetishes and other magical accoutrements.

This tradition of using words of power continued from late antiquity (the provenance of the *PGM*) to the Middle Ages and the Renaissance. We can find words of power in the grimoires of the *Picatrix, Keys of Solomon, Ars Notoria, Sworn Book of Honorius*, and many others, including Dee's Enochian language used in his diaries. These words of power seem to be corruptions of names of deities and angels and sacred terms and phrases in various languages, but from the standpoint of the ritual magician, they have no intrinsic meaning other than the pure expression of magical power in a verbal construct. This is why scholars have given these words the label *verba ignota*, since in many cases their actual source and meaning are indeterminable.

The fact that the magician is speaking these words and doesn't know their meanings seems to have little impact on their use and reputed powers. A magician could completely make up a language and profess that it comes from a hitherto unknown ancient source, and as long as it sounds impressive and exotic, it will have an unprecedented power in the mind of the wielder. Such is the way of the barbarous words of power: their meaning is not as important as their sound and perceived esthetic value. However, while these words of power are being expressed forcefully by the magician, they have an intention and a latent semantic value, based on the context in the ritual they are used, that contains the implied meaning of these words. Words of power, therefore, mean whatever the magician believes that they mean, and within the context of a magical working, this is all that is needed to express their implicit meaning.

NOTARY ART OF MAGIC

I have assembled all of the techniques I have listed in this introduction as belonging to *the notary art of magic*. The notary art is a method of writing or producing an occult language that has meaning and significance within the spirit world, and therefore has a certain power and mystery in the mundane world.

At a glance, these symbols, markings, seals, signatures, nota, and words of power are peculiar oddities that seem to be meaningless, opaque, and even nonsensical to the untrained. That a person must learn various methodologies and techniques to make these occult systems of communication sensible and intelligibly significant are the very layers that make them obscure but also make them esthetically powerful and magically useful. These are tools of communication, but they generate messages to a world that is beyond logic and rational thought, where symbols and signs are living representations for actual material things and occurrences.

This world is the domain of Spirit, found above the plane of the eye of flesh and mind. It is a place where there is a direct correspondence between dreams, ideas, and concepts, and the material things that they represent. It is the transformational plane where thought becomes form and form becomes thought, and it is intertwined with a language of symbols, signs, names, and exhortations or words of power. It is the place where spirits and deities reside, and where the energies of magic and miracles are found. This interstice is the place where magic can impact the mental and material worlds—but not always in accordance with the will of the magician.

We live with one foot in this world and the other in the material world, and our mind attempts to bridge the differences and resolve their duality. Yet only when the mind is briefly untethered to the material world can it realize the full potency and significance of this world. Beyond even this world, which I call the *domain of Spirit* or the *super symbolic reality*, one can find the means to resolve duality into a unitary expression of consciousness, which some have called the *sphere of enlightenment*. What occurs in the spirit world has its origin in this world, where everything is unified into a single and unknowable source.

INFORMATION MODEL AND INFORMATION THEORY

If the notary art represents the communication between the worlds of mind, matter, and spirit, then it must obey certain rules and contain certain structures. A recent theory about this mechanism can be found in the information model of magic as originally developed in chaos magic, although there are two different perspectives on this model, based on either a purely linguistic or semantic definition of magic or the theory of communication itself.

The information model of magic contains the linguistic phenomenon of the communication of information, although it is limited to the communication process of meaning within a magical context. However, that definition extends to everything that magicians employ to work their magic, including the symbols, correspondences, regalia, tools, rituals, and intentions that make up a magical rite. That communication of information, seen as packets of data moving sequentially through multiple streams of consciousness from our world to the spirit world and then back again, is the primal media of magic. All of this data orbits around the magician's intention, which enters into the world of Spirit and returns or echoes back as the manifesting wave of that magic.

Patrick Dunn introduced the initial idea of the information model of magic back in 1987, and some proponents of this methodology, those who practice what they call *cybermagic*, believe that this is the only model of note. Of course, we know this to be an exaggeration because the other models are still important representations of magical methodologies. The intrinsic meaning of ideas and words represent a semantic deep structure that has an equivalence in both worlds, so it becomes important to fully understand the etymology of a word to determine its true meaning and significance. This approach could also involve the discipline of semiotics, particularly the study and analysis of what is referred to as *post-language signs*.

Perhaps the best approach is the one that Scott Stenwick developed, where he applied the information model of magic to information theory, making it more straightforward and easier to realize. According to Stenwick, there are three components to information theory: the message, the carrier, and the transmission. This model is particularly well adapted to understanding the building of an important magical artifact, the magical link.[1]

Using communication theory and applying it to magic, the message is, of course, the objective or intention for this work.

---

1 See the online blog *Augoeides: Spiritual Technology for a New Aeon* for the article "Regarding Magical Models Part 10" by Scott Stenwick. http://ananael.blogspot.com/2016/11/regarding-magical-models-part-ten.html. Accessed March 26, 2024.

This is what the magician seeks to express or communicate to the spirit world. Magical energy is the carrier that sends or moves the message, and the transmission is the line or link between the worlds. An effective magical operation will have a clear message, an energized carrier, and the proper line of transmission between the worlds (or between the subject and the target of the working).

A magical message needs to be translated into a proper symbolic construct that is meaningful in the spirit world, since it will be traveling to that world in order to be interpreted. The line of transmission is established through the operator's spiritual alignment, developed through their liturgical work and the fact that they reside in both worlds. I have found that being immersed in the spirit world and having the capacity to visualize and sense that domain greatly helps establish the transmission line between worlds.

A weakness in any of the three components will greatly reduce the efficacy of the magical working. Also, a more compressed and condensed message will be able to pack more information into it, making it more effective. This is where sigils, seals, signatures, symbols, and notae are the most effective means of translating the message into its most condensed formulation. Because of the occult nature of sigils, they can function as both the message and the line of transmission, since they bridge both worlds. What is required, then, is a source of energy to function as the carrier.

This is where the idea of the information model working by itself seems to fail, because there is the requirement in information theory for some kind of energy to function as the carrier. What is needed to fully make this magical model comply with the information theory is some kind of energy field that would be used to push the message along the line of transmission. Whether that energy field is generated magically through the use of bodily raised energy (like movement and breath) or through a more complex procedure, such as elemental magic, some kind of energy needs to be raised to energize the message. Sigils by themselves don't possess the energy required for the carrier, so it must be supplied externally by the operator. Sigils can represent the message and the line of transmission, but otherwise, they are dormant, latent potentials without an effective energy body.

There are two ways that a sigil becomes activated: through empowering them in a rite or by consecration. Empowering a sigil is simply using it in a magical working that has an energy field raised in some fashion. Consecration sacralizes a sigil through the context of a magical and liturgical exercise, where it is exposed to sacraments (oil, lustral water, or incense) and blessed by a combination of sign, breath, and focused intention. A consecrated sigil could function on its own because it has been energized and empowered, but it is often used in a magical operation, where it absorbs an even greater field of energy.

Consecrating and empowering a sigil activates the message and the process of transmission, making it possible to communicate the message. Energy provides the body for the sigil, causing it to become an activated sign or symbol in the spirit world. Whether that sigil represents the specific signature of a spirit or the desire or objective of the magician, it establishes a link between the magician as subject and the target, allowing for further work to be performed, such as an invocation, evocation, or projected materialization or exteriorization of intent.

It doesn't matter if the main magical working is employing the spirit model, energy model, or the psychological model: building and deploying the magical link between subject and object through the domain of Spirit is integral to all forms of successful magic. It is also where the magic fails when any of the components of the link are weak, missing, or poorly defined.

A BOOK ON SIGIL MAGIC: THE NOTARY ART

As you can see, the discipline of sigil magic covers a number of different methodologies and techniques. It is not one single method, but many. Some of the techniques have a historical provenance, making them part of the practice of magic that has passed through the ages from our ancestors' hands to ours. Other techniques are more modern and have been used only recently with our post-modern perspectives. Some of these techniques, such as building and using notae or diagrams consisting of angelic and deity names, have not been used since medieval times. Yet all these methods and techniques must be brought into the singular modern practice of a ritual magician in order to be fully realized. Often, a magician will employ one or two of them and forget the rest, but there is value in at least knowing all the different types of the notary art.

While there are books in print that one might purchase to make these different methodologies available to one's magical work, there is no single book that includes a discussion and encapsulation of all these different types of magical operations. What I have done is publish a book that examines sigil magic as a complete discipline of magic, naming it the notary art so that it can include current and ancient methodologies to cover the spectrum of these techniques. Yet I also aspire to be brief and concise so that this book is not an overly large work. To facilitate a more condensed approach, I will, in some cases, refer the reader to other works already in print, but I will at least briefly cover that methodology and show how it is valuable to the practice of a modern ritual magician.

This book is a singular work that will act as compendium of magical techniques and a reference work for the notary art of magic. It will be the first place that a magician searches to discover a technique that they might wish to employ in their magical workings. If that technique requires a considerable amount of background material, then I will at least discuss that technique to some depth and refer the reader to another more comprehensive work, noting the chapters and pages that one would study.

Some of the techniques presented here require many pages and chapters to fully explain them, and I feel that at least fairly representing them in this book with references and citations should suffice to give the student a complete background on that particular topic. At the very least, I will show how many of the techniques of the notary art of magic can be employed in one's magical workings and discuss their importance in the discipline of modern practical magic. Through this approach, one will at least be familiar with them.

In writing this book, I have strategically examined the basic techniques needed to work all forms of magic using the notary art of magic. Therefore, this book seeks to encompass the various techniques of sigil magic in four basic parts. I have divided sigil magic into two different groupings: sigils and seals that represent the names of spirits, and sigils that represent aspirations and objectives, such as Spare's system of sigil magic, magical alphabets, and magical notae (like what is found in the grimoire *Ars Notoria*). Two additional parts will examine the methods for sigil consecration and charging, and how to employ sigils in magical workings. The contents of this book will completely cover the different techniques and methods for employing sigils and seals in one's magical rites, thus becoming the definitive work on the notary art of magic.

This work was written for the established practitioner of magic and is, therefore, not a beginner's book. If you are a beginner who doesn't have experience working magic, then it is likely that this book will be a bit beyond your abilities to make practical use of it. However, I do have a book recommendation for beginners that employs sigil magic for imprinting magically raised energy: *Mastering the Art of Witchcraft*. Acquiring that book and using it to build up a magical and liturgical practice, incorporating sigils in your magical workings, will give you the experience required to tackle the topics in this book. In Chapter Four of *Mastering the Art of Witchcraft*, the section "Sigil Magic, Signs, Seals, and Witch Marks" should enable a beginner to gain enough knowledge and practical experience to make this book accessible.[2]

Here is how I have structured this work for the benefit of my readers:

- **Part I** examines the methodologies and techniques of applying sigils or seals to the identities of spirits for the purpose of empowering the rites of invocation and evocation. We will look first at the methods of using magical squares and briefly discuss the art of Kamea or magical square magic and how they can be used to

---

2 Frater Barrabbas, *Mastering the Art of Witchcraft* (Crossed Crow Books, 2024).

derive sigils and seals. This will be a brief examination since it is a technique that I don't employ in my own magic. We will then move on to discuss using alphabet wheels to develop sigils in any language, and then how to construct magical seals that are a major part of the famous grimoires produced in the renaissance and later. Seals such as those used in the grimoire *Lemegeton* of the Goetia were invented by someone at some time, and likely were embellished over time to be represented as we see them today. What this means is that we can create our own seals, so we will examine the techniques used to achieve that task.

- **Part II** examines the methodologies and techniques of symbolizing aspirations and magical objectives. Austin Spare came up with his own method for symbolizing the targets of his magic and even encapsulated phrases and expressions into hieroglyphic and pictographic sigils. This spawned a whole new approach to the art of sigil magic, and it is one of the most useful systems ever developed. We will examine this methodology in detail since it is easy to learn and deploy in one's magic. Yet Spare's system was very unique in that it can be used to create graphic representations as well as fashion words of power or mantras. We will look at words of power and how they were used over the ages and show how this art can be employed by magicians today. Additionally, we will examine different magical alphabets, briefly discuss the building of formulas and acronyms through letter substitution, and analyze the techniques of translating letters to numbers and numbers to letters. We will also look at the lost art of notae and how modern magicians might employ this medieval artform in their magical work.

- **Part III** examines the techniques for consecrating and charging sigils and seals, making them fully active and capable of functioning as surrogates for the names of spirits or empowering a magical link to achieve an objective. Knowing how to develop and construct a sigil or seal is only the first step in the methodology of employing them for magic.

- **Part IV** examines the various methods of employing sigils, seals, signatures, and notae to build magical links, identify spirits, and empower aspirations and materialize objectives. Sigils and seals can be deployed in a number of different kinds of magical workings, using the magical models of spirit, energy, psychology, and even the temporal model of magic used to generate talismans. Sigils are an integral part of most magical operations, and once consecrated and charged, they can also be used by themselves to achieve a magical objective. This final part will readily demonstrate the ubiquity and utility of the notary art.

As you can see, this book will bring together—perhaps for the first time—all of the techniques and methodologies where occult symbols and ideograms of some sort can be realized, constructed, and employed in the art of magic. I believe that these numerous techniques should be once again grouped together and named the notary art, since they are an integral part of the communication between worlds and the mechanism used to translate, materialize, and objectify the beings and powers associated with art of magic. Let us now proceed to examine all of these techniques so that we will have the greatest possible outcome in the magic we wield.

PART I

SIGILS, SEALS, AND SIGNATURES FOR SPIRITS

CHAPTER ONE

BRIEF DISCUSSION ABOUT PLANETARY KAMEAS AND MAGIC SQUARES

IN THIS CHAPTER, WE WILL DISCUSS the use of sigil, seals, signatures, and marks that represent the essence and identity of spirits. Being able to build and use sigils that represent the identity of a spirit in a symbolic manner is a critical skill used in the art of spirit conjuration. A ritual magician will employ a sigil when a seal for a given entity is not known. Once a spirit has been invoked, as part of the constraining and binding or communion steps, the operator will seek to get the spirit to reveal its seal, mark, and signature to add to the sigil as a symbolic means of identifying it. Once a consecrated seal or mark is constructed, the spirit can be summoned through that established link without having to undergo a lengthier invocation or evocation working. We will examine the methods and techniques for constructing sigils, seals, signatures, and marks in this chapter as an important feature of the notary art.

While I know more than enough to be dangerous working with magical squares and deriving sigils and seals from them, this is not a methodology that I personally use in my magic. That being said, I can still discuss them from a theoretical and practical perspective, and I can steer you to other sources that deal with the matter in greater detail. What I can say is that magical squares are a discipline and a magical artform that has an extensive body of lore and represents an entire area of study all by itself. It is also one the oldest methodologies for producing seals and sigils, and I base that on the fact that Agrippa discusses it in his three-part book *Occult Philosophy*, and it also shown in the *Book of Abramelin*. I only learned about these other methodologies later in my studies, so I developed simpler methods to derive a sigil because I lacked any documentation on the more complicated approaches. We will examine some of the basic features of the magic square regarding their use in constructing sigils and seals.

Magical squares are tables that contain an equal, even, or odd number of columns and rows, producing a number of internal cells to which numbers, letters, or a combination of them are inserted. This widespread art can be found in the Middle East, Europe, and Asia, and has an ancient provenance. In Hebrew, a magic square is called a *Kamea* (*Qamya'a,* root *QMH,* "to gather"), which is loosely translated as a written or lettered amulet or talisman.

According to Nineveh Shadrach, there are four types of magical squares.[3] These use a combination of number only, alphabetic and numeric alternated, alphabetic only, and a mixture of letters and numbers. Magical squares are typically deployed solely as magical tools and based on similar practices today, they would be constructed during an auspicious astrological time and place, then consecrated. A magic square can be used to translate magical powers, channel spirits, and even imprint the mind of the operator with spiritual and occult knowledge. They do not have to be used to construct sigils or seals, and they are typically used either with magical workings or by themselves as a complete and concise magical working. A great example of magical squares used to perform magical operations are the squares associated with the Abramelin working.

The simplest example of a magic square has three columns and rows, labeled a magic square of the order 3, or 3 squared. In magical literature, there are seven orders listed: 3, 4, 5, 6, 7, 8, and 9.[4] While there are magical squares with many more columns and rows than these seven, these are more often used because they are the seven

---

3   Shadrach, Nineveh, *The Occult Encyclopedia of Magic Squares: Planetary Angels and Spirits of Ceremonial Magic* (Ishtar Publishing, 2009) p. iii.

4   Shadrach, Nineveh, *The Occult Encyclopedia of Magic Squares: Planetary Angels and Spirits of Ceremonial Magic* (Ishtar Publishing, 2009) p. x.

magic squares of the seven planets of antiquity. The seven planets are actually the Sun and Moon, along with the five non-Earth planets known of at the time: Saturn, Jupiter, Mars, Venus, and Mercury. They are ordered from the slowest moving planet to the fastest based on the Ptolemaic planetary sequence, which also matches with the planets associated with the seven Sephiroth of the Qabalah, notably Yesod upward on the Tree of Life through Binah.

Shadrach, in his book, also showed how to use an order 4 square to define the sixteen elemental spirits used in a number of magical approaches.[5] I found this approach to be quite brilliant, since I am a proponent of using planets and elements together to forge the talismanic field. The use of magical squares is as unlimited as the mathematical mind combined with the power of imagination—the number of possibilities is nearly endless. While interesting, we will limit our discussion of them and focus on how they can be employed to create sigils and seals.

We can organize the magical squares as demonstrated above, thereby covering the full spectrum of magical qualities for the seven planets, four elements, and the twelve signs of the zodiac. We will focus on the planetary squares and briefly discuss how they might be used in magical operations. The operator can choose to make use of those known sigils and seals as they are found in occult and magical literature, or they can decide to construct the squares and then design the required sigils and seals from them. If you are going to use this methodology to symbolically identify spirits, then I would recommend fully studying the background materials for these squares and seek to fully comprehend and master their use.

Here is my list of magical squares and their associations. These kinds of magic squares are numeric, and they require the ability to translate letters into numbers and reduce like numbers into a number that is included in the cell of the magic square (for instance, 30 could be replaced with 3, or 100 with 10 or 1). For more complex and larger squares, the introduction of multiple letters or phrases becomes appropriate.

---

5 Shadrach, Nineveh, *The Occult Encyclopedia of Magic Squares: Planetary Angels and Spirits of Ceremonial Magic* (Ishtar Publishing, 2009) p. xii.

LIST OF MAGICAL SQUARES
AND THEIR ATTRIBUTIONS

3 x 3	4 x 4	5 x 5
Saturn	Jupiter	Mars
6 x 6	7 x 7	8 x 8
Sun	Venus	Mercury
9 x 9	4 x 4	12 x 12
Moon	Four Elements	Zodiac

Translating letters to numbers and numbers to letters is part of the system of Qabalah known as *Gematria*. The source of this system is likely Greek, since letters in Classical Greek were also used to define numbers. Classical Hebrew (and, similarly, Arabic) had the same system of numbers being represented by letters. In this manner, the letters found within a word can be added up to calculate a number value for that word. Thus, different words could have the name number and thereby be considered related in an occult manner.

However, the use of letter substitution and acronym building are considered a part of the techniques of Temurah and Notariqan. Notariqon is a system of building or exploding acronyms. Temurah is a system of letter permutation or substitution, and there are two types. The first methodology uses the Hebrew alphabet broken in half so that eleven letters are paired, and one letter is substituted with the other letter of the pair. There are a number of different eleven letter pairings that can act as a cypher. The second method of substitution uses a table of nine cells (3 x 3), where letters are grouped according to their numeric value, such as A, Y and Q, which have the values of 1, 10, and 100, respectively. Using the magic squares requires a system of letter to number substitutions, and this is where the second method of Temurah is utilized.

The first example we will examine to help illustrate this approach to magical squares uses the idea that the twenty-two letters of the Hebrew alphabet each have an associated number or numeric value. Those letters with a final form (as opposed to beginning or medial positions as they appear in words) that also changes the shape of the letters will have an extra number ranging in the hundreds. If a name of a spirit is to be associated with a magical square, then those numbers may need to be reduced so that they can match the numbers in the square.

Here is the Hebrew alphabet with each letter's associated numeric values.

Name	Letter	Value	Name	Letter	Value
Aleph	א	1	Samekh	ס	60
Beth	ב	2	Ayin	ע	70
Gimel	ג	3	Peh	פ	80
Daleth	ד	4	Tzaddi	צ	90
Heh	ה	5	Qoph	ק	100
Vav	ו	6	Resh	ר	200
Zain	ז	7	Shin	ש	300
Cheth	ח	8	Tav	ת	400
Teth	ט	9	Final Kaph	ך	500
Yod	י	10	Final Mem	ם	600
Kaph	כ	20	Final Nun	ן	700
Lamed	ל	30	Final Peh	ף	800
Mem	מ	40	Final Tzaddi	ץ	900
Nun	נ	50			

Using this table, we can easily determine the numeric value each of the letters in a spirit name (provided that it is transliterable to the Hebrew alphabet), and we can add up those numbers to determine the combined value and then compare that to a list of like words with the same number, as in Gematria, or we seek to apply them to one of the planetary square to derive a sigil that can represent the spirit in a linear graphic design. To adjust the number values of the letters of a name, we will use the method of Temurah called *AIQ BKR* or the Qabalah of Nine Chambers.[6]

Let us present a puzzle using this method of letter substitution. Suppose we want to determine the sigil for the angelic spirit of Saturn named ZAZL or Zazel. If we look at each of the numbers associated with each letter, we will get the numbers 7, 1, 7, and 30. We want to draw a linear graphic structure over the planetary square of Saturn, which has an order of 3. However, the highest number on the planetary square of Saturn is 9, so the number 30 could not be placed anywhere on the square. In order to overcome that difficulty, we will use the AIQ BKR table in the third cell to the top right to exchange the letter L (30) for the letter G (3), which allows us to map it to the planetary square. That method of substitution is how one could approach deriving a sigil for a planetary spirit.

Each chamber contains three letters representing the same associated numbers in a factor of ten. So, Gimel, Daleth, and Shin occupy the same third cell, representing the numbers 3, 30, and 300. Letter substitution allows the operator to find the letter and numeric value that will fit in a number-only magical square. Substituting can also change the meaning of the name, so in this case Zazel becomes Zazeg, which doesn't have any meaning in Hebrew, but some substitutions might also change the meaning of the name.

On the next page is an example of the AIQ BKR or the Table of Nine Chambers.

---

6   Crowley, Aleister, *777 and other Writings of Aleister Crowley* (Samuel Weiser, 1973) p. 4.

Gimel	ג	3	Beth	ב	2	Aleph	א	1
Lamen	ל	30	Kaph	כ	20	Yod	י	10
Shin	ש	300	Resh	ר	200	Qoph	ק	100
Vav	ו	6	Heh	ה	5	Daleth	ד	4
Samekh	ס	60	Nun	נ	50	Mem	מ	40
Final Mem	ם	600	Final Kaph	ך	500	Tav	ת	400
Teth	ט	9	Cheth	ח	8	Zain	ז	7
Tzaddi	צ	90	Peh	פ	80	Ayin	ע	70
Final Tzaddi	ץ	900	Final Peh	ף	800	Final Nun	ן	700

Here is an example of the sigil of ZAZL drawn on the planetary square of Saturn.

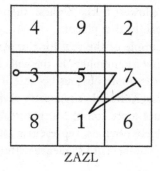

ZAZL

As you can see, the linear movement of the sigil goes from right to left, same as the direction of reading a Hebrew word or phrase. The Z cell of 7 is repeated twice between the A cell of 1; sometimes this is done with a curling loop if the letter is repeated twice with no letter in between. All of the letters, translated to numbers, are connected together to form a linear graphic structure. Such a sigil is a line with a beginning and an end, which can be determined with a crossing line at the beginning and a circle or arrow at the end. Note, though, that the act of creating a sigil is an artistic representation. Making sigils is an art form, and while there are basic rules that one should follow, so the artist as magician can use their imagination and sense of esthetics to embellish and elaborate a simple sigil.

Of course, what I have shown you using Zazel against the planetary square of Saturn is the easiest representation of the craft of sigil and seal construction using the planetary squares. However, this is the basic mechanism used to produce sigils on the planetary squares to represent planetary spirits and angels. One would use the same mechanism for plotting sigils against the larger and more complex magical squares. Since the larger squares also have more possible number variations, one could use multiple letters grouped together to target numbers in the square as well as the individual letters.

The planetary seals are based on the numerical sequence of the planetary squares. If we draw a series of lines that follow the numbers from the lowest to the highest, then the derived linear structure is the seal for that planet.

Here is an example of the seal for the planet Saturn based on lines that follow the numbers in the cells from 1 through 9. While that might be more obvious because it is the simplest of the planetary squares, the other planetary seals follow the same pattern but produce more complex structures. These seals, while not being intuitively obvious, represent a creative solution to covering all of the numbers in a sequence within the magic square.

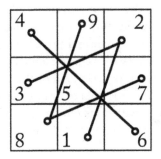

There can be a number of different solutions that would produce a seal that obeys the rules to cover the entire sequence of numbers. This is why I would advise students to use the seals as they have been derived by Agrippa and others, established over the centuries as the form represented for that planet. This doesn't negate any degree of experimentation or discovering other examples that meet the same requirements. It is necessary to fully understand how the planetary squares are derived and developed in order to derive the sigils and seals for planetary spirits or, in the case of seals, for the planet as a complete and holistic representation.[7]

Magical squares for the seven planets, the four elements, and the twelve zodiacal signs, along with a plethora of other types and examples, are a distinct and separate discipline of magic that requires extensive research and study to master. They can be used to draw the sigils for the names of spirits, but it requires that these spirits be directly associated with the qualities of that planet, element, or zodiacal sign. While it is possible to sort various types of spirits into these classifications, it is not always practical. It is for this reason that I do not use magic squares to derive sigils for the spirits that I may decide to conjure. Many spirits do not fit into these nice and neat categories, and some of them cannot be adequately represented by Hebrew spelling since they have a Greek or Latin language origin. Hebrew has twenty-two letters, all consonants, Greek has twenty-four, and Latin twenty-one. Not all letters in one language are comparable to the letters in another language. Examples would be the Hebrew letters Ain, Shin, and Chet, and the letters Tet and Tau, which are often difficult to render from Greek or Latin to Hebrew.

There are quite a range of different spirits from various grimoires that do not fit into these categories and whose names are not easily spelled using the Hebrew alphabet. To be able to construct sigils for these spirits requires a completely different approach, and we

---

7   See Tyson, Donald, editor, *Three Books of Occult Philosophy written by Henry Cornelius Agrippa of Nettesheim* (Llewellyn Publications, 1992) pp. 733–751 for a complete analysis of magic squares, sigils, and seals as shown in the third book.

will be looking at this in the next chapter. What is best practiced, in my opinion, is to have a methodology that is flexible enough to accommodate any language that might be used to spell the name of a spirit. Some spirits have obvious Hebrew names (especially if they have an -AL or -YH ending), but others may have names that are of Greek origin, and still others seem to be a Latin or even English spelling, so it would be important to be able to manage a name that can exist in any language. There is the difficulty in determining vowels when attempting to spell a name with vowels in Hebrew, which makes the whole process complicated.

However, since the art of magical squares is an entirely distinct magical discipline, and if this magical methodology appeals to you, then learning the art of creating sigils and seals becomes an important skill to master. Of course, that would also indicate that other sources and resources of this type of magic would be necessary since I will not elucidate them in this work. Instead, I will point my readers to other resources here if they are keen to learn and master this excellent magical discipline.

First of all, Nineveh Shadrach's book *The Occult Encyclopedia of Magic Squares* is a comprehensive resource for magic squares and their use as a magical tool. This is a veritable doorstop volume that contains magical squares to contact, summon, and channel a massive list of spirits associated with the planets, signs of the zodiac, elements, and decans. If you are interested in how to use magical squares to invoke spirits, then Shadrach's book will provide you with everything that you might want to know.

Another good resource for understanding how the planetary squares are constructed is to be found in Appendix 5 of Donald Tyson's book *Three Books of Occult Philosophy*, translated from the Latin originally written by Agrippa. The appendix spans the pages from 733 to 751 and is an excellent examining of Agrippa's use of the planetary magical squares.

I would also recommend the book *777 and Other Qabalistic Writings of Aleister Crowley*, where Crowley discusses the different methodologies of Gematria, Notariqon, and, most importantly, the second method of Temurah, were he expounds on the AIQ BKR table and shows how it is used. You can find this section of the book located on pages 1 through 50. I have also written about this method of Temurah in my book *Magical Qabalah for Beginners* and included the methods for producing the sigil of Zazel using the AIQ BKR. You can find that information located on pages 293 through 297.

Finally, Sara Mastros covers this topic quite well in her online course "Introduction to Witchcraft," lesson three, Symbols, Seals, and Sigils. This lesson will be incorporated into her introductory book on magic with the same title to be published in October 2025 by Crossed Crow Books.

CHAPTER TWO

ALPHABET WHEELS: HEBREW, GREEK, AND LATIN

THE METHOD THAT I EMPLOY EXCLUSIVELY for producing a sigil from a spirit's name is using an alphabet wheel, and then drawing the sigil over the letter positions in that wheel. This is such an easy method to produce spirit name sigils, but the mystery is how I eventually figured out how to do this task. It was purely by chance, since I am not always very observant and methodical in my approach to studying and reading about magical techniques. That is probably why I didn't carefully read the lesson on Sigils in the Golden Dawn as found in book seven of that collection. Because I glossed over that section, I didn't realize the fact that the center of the Rose Cross emblem on the Golden Dawn Rose Cross tool was in fact an alphabet wheel of the Hebrew alphabet.

It wasn't until the great doorstop edition of the Golden Dawn book was published in the early 1980s that the Rose Cross Hebrew alphabet wheel was shown along with the sigils generated by tracing the lines of a Hebrew angel name over the cells of that wheel.[8] It was only then that I made the connection and began using that large illustration of the alphabet wheel and tracing paper to draw the sigils that I needed. It was easy, efficient to use, and worked, so once I had that tool as part of my repertoire, I never needed to

---

8 Regardie, Israel, *The Complete Golden Dawn System of Magic*, p. 39. This was the door-stop edition, volume five.

master the art of magical squares. I would recommend that you acquire a copy of that book and study the lesson on sigils in book seven of the Golden Dawn book.[9]

However, I also discovered that there were some limitations to using the Hebrew alphabet wheel. Every name I wanted to translate into a sigil had to be spelled out using Hebrew letters, and translating vowels became an issue. It wasn't a problem when the spirit names were of obvious Hebrew origin, but there are some spirits whose names are not easily spelled using Hebrew letters, particularly if their roots were Greek or Latin.

Hebrew Alphabet Wheel

The alphabet wheel was a remarkable device that took the Hebrew letters and distributed them onto three concentric rings within a circle that was divided into cells for the three mother letters (A, M, Sh), the seven double letters (B, D, G, K, P, R, Th) and the twelve single letters, (H, V, Z, Ch, T, Y, L, N, S, Ain, TZ, Q), which could also correspond to the three elements, seven planets, and twelve signs of the zodiac. Thus, the inner ring has three cells, the second ring has seven cells, and the third and outer ring has twelve cells. All these letters function as consonants, where

---

9   Regardie, Israel, *The Golden Dawn 7th Edition* (Llewellyn Publications, 2016) pp. 608–611, 622–643. This is the latest version of the GD materials. It does not have the Hebrew alphabet wheel diagram.

the vowels were later determined by markings notated below the letters, likely borrowed from the vowel notation used in Arabic.

As I have stated, this alphabet wheel is a great tool, but it is limited to the Hebrew letters. I understood that alphabet wheels could be more useful if I would apply this same kind of structure to other alphabets, most notably Greek and Latin. The Greek alphabet also has three natural groupings: the seven vowels, eight semi-vowels, and nine voiceless consonants for a total of twenty-four letters. I created three concentric rings like the Hebrew alphabetic wheel, but the inner ring had seven divisions, the second ring had eight, and the third and outer ring had nine cells. I was able to develop this alphabet wheel and place the Greek letters into the cells.

Greek Alphabet Wheel

The English alphabet has five vowels, nine voiced consonants, and twelve voiceless consonants, for a total of twenty-six letters. Latin is similar to English because both have five vowels, but only sixteen consonants remain, for a total of twenty-one letters (or twenty-three, with eighteen consonants, after the conquering of Greece). However, I felt that the English alphabet wheel would adequately cover for Latin words and could also be used for many European spirit names with a simple spelling technique. With these insights, I was able to create a Greek alphabet wheel and an English/Latin alphabet wheel, and I could use these to produce sigils for any spirit name that I chose to represent in this manner.

English/Latin Alphabet Wheel

Armed with the knowledge of these alphabet wheels, I made them large enough to use in the construction of sigils. By placing tracing paper over the alphabet wheel, I could easily design and produce a valid sigil representation of the spirit's name. While some might state that using magic squares is more authentic and has a historical use behind them, I have found that alphabet wheels are also powerful magical artifacts that can be used to fashion a magical tool or emblem of one's magical tradition. The Alexandrians used the Rose Ankh and placed an alphabet wheel in its roseate center, although it was one that was based on the Gaelic alphabet. I do have copy of it, given to me as supposed oath-bound material when I achieved the third degree, but I have no practical use for it, so it is not something that I would show here even if I could.

CONSTRUCTING SIGILS USING ALPHABET WHEELS

If you wish to employ alphabet wheels in your magical workings, you should first construct all three wheels using heavy construction paper or tag board. You should also acquire a compass, 180-degree or 360-degree protractor, drafting triangles (small and large), various drafting templates, an eraser, pencils and various calligraphic pens and Magic Markers, scissors, and an X-Acto knife. For talismans, I like to get a good grade of parchment paper and a pad of tracing paper. You will find that these tools are inexpensive, but they are an important part of the tool kit that a magician uses for many of their graphical magical endeavors. An important note: I always use light pencil lines when laying out the form of the design before committing it to ink.

To construct the alphabet wheel, use a compass or a circle template of a suitable size and draw the outer ring. Then draw the three inner concentric rings with equal amounts of space between them. The very center of the four concentric circles should be a circle that is left blank. The three rings will be divided into cells where letters will be printed.

The Hebrew alphabet wheel has three divisions to construct in the three concentric rings, with the inner circle left blank. The inner ring is divided into three sections, so, using your protractor, you will mark out points that are 120 degrees equidistant and then divide that ring into three cells, drawing the dividing lines to the imaginary point in the center.

The second ring will have seven divisions, so you will use your protractor to make marks on the circle every 51.5 degrees or so. Then, draw the lines in the second ring using the imaginary point in the center of the circle to align them.

The third and outer ring will have twelve divisions, so you will use your protractor to make marks on the circle every 30 degrees, then draw the lines in the third ring using the imaginary point in the center of the circle to align them.

You now have the wheel constructed in pencil, so you will need to go over the design with a pen using the templates or compass and a triangle to draw the lines that define the cells in each of the rings. Once that is done, you can use a pen to fill in the cells with either the Hebrew letters (or use the equivalent English letters) and produce a Hebrew alphabet wheel resembling my example above. Make certain that the circles, lines, and letters are dark enough to be easily seen through tracing paper.

A Greek alphabet wheel has a different number of cells for each ring, so the markings that you will make with your protractor will be different. Otherwise, it is the same four concentric circles forming three rings. The inner ring will employ markings every 51.5 degrees for the seven divisions, the second ring will employ markings every 45 degrees for eight, and the third will employ markings every 40 degrees for nine divisions. Once you have constructed the wheel with those divisions in the three rings, then you can write the letters in the cell, copying the image above. You can use Greek letters or the English equivalent.

For the third and final English/Latin alphabet wheel, the markings would be 72 degrees for the inner ring, 40 degrees for the second ring, and 30 degrees for the outer ring, making five, nine, and twelve segments for each of the three rings, respectively. Once the wheel is constructed, then you can add the letters of the English alphabet in the manner shown above.

If you construct the wheels from tag board or heavy paper, then they might be too fragile to use as magical tools. However, if you use plywood boards, then you can consecrate the alphabet wheels and they will become magical tools. If you are going to use the wheels as magical tools, then I would use the Hebrew and Greek alphabets for the best effect, and you could also paint the boards, painting the wheels interesting contrasting colors to create a powerful visual effect. Making sigils using a consecrated alphabet wheel would give the overall process a much more potent efficacy, making it a part of the magic that you employ to symbolize, identify, and sacralize the magical link between a spirit and the material world.

DRAWING AND MAKING SPIRIT SIGILS

Once you have the alphabet wheels constructed and ready for use, you will be able to make a sigil from a spirit's name. Knowing the name of a spirit is very important. If you don't have a name, then you don't have an identity or a way to call and conjure the spirit. There are a vast number of spirits just in the environment around you, but the important ones will cluster around various features in your environment. Local spirits will have to be identified in some manner, and you can typically find their names through various forms of divination.

Sometimes, the easiest way is to ask them to give you their name while in a semi-trance state. You would have to go to where you think they reside and sit very still next to that feature, be it a tree, hill, lake, well, or even a tall building or city park. Go there, sit quietly and unobtrusively, and assume a quiet and light trance state. Then, probe the area with your eyes and imagination, close your eyes, listen carefully, and, in your mind, ask that spirit whoever is there to reveal themselves to you. Ask them for their name and see if you get an answer. You might need to use divination as an aid, and I found that a pendulum held over an alphabet wheel can sometimes help get a spirit's name. Determining the source language for that name might be challenging once given, since many locations can have many layers of language associated with them, as the place names in the US that span both European and Native American languages would seem to indicate.

If you are going to use a traditional source of spirit names, such as a grimoire or a spirit list from some occult or religious tradition, then you will first determine what language alphabet wheel you might use to build a sigil for that spirit name. If the name ends in -AL or -YH, then it is likely Hebrew. (In that case, if you also have the Hebrew spelling, that would be even better.) A large percentage of angelic names are of Hebrew extraction. However, Goetic demons and other kinds of spirits in traditions other than Solomonic would likely be Greek or Latin. If it is Greek, then like Hebrew, get the Greek spelling. If you don't have a clue, then use the English wheel. The whole point of this exercise is to produce a sigil that you can use to summon a spirit. For instance, I prefer to use the English wheel to construct sigils for the various Enochian spirits, since that was the primary language that Dee used in his magical work.

When I use the Hebrew alphabet wheel, I like to sequentially plot the letters on the wheel moving from right to left, simply because the language is written that way, but it actually doesn't make too much difference if you have exchanged the Hebrew alphabet for the English one. Place a piece of tracing paper over the wheel and plot out the letters of the name with pencil. You can use a drafting triangle to make the lines straight and true. At the beginning of the linear sigil, positioning on the first letter, I draw a cross over the end of the line, showing that this is where the sigil structure points to the first letter in the name. You could also use a small circle. Then, I plot the name of the wheel, drawing lines from one letter cell to another until the name is spelled in the linear form. I can draw an arrow at the end or just leave it unmarked; either way will suffice. If a letter is repeated, then you can make a squiggle or spring like line going back and forth between the cell of the doubled letter.

So, there are three steps to drawing a sigil on an alphabet wheel. The first is to plot the line from letter to letter, then draw a smaller crossing line over the line for the first character, and then draw an arrow at the end of the line for the last character. Let me give you an example of how to draw a sigil for the Goetic spirit Vasago, which would be spelled VShAGV in Hebrew. For this sigil, the beginning of the line is in the same cell as the end, forming an interesting looking sigil that reminds me of a lightning bolt.

Once you have drawn the sigil on tracing paper, remove it and use a marker to draw the lines as heavy and dark as possible so that it will be seen when tracing it on a piece of parchment paper first with a pencil, then with an ink pen. You might also put some other identification on the parchment, such as the spirit's name and any other correspondence that will help you to identify the spirit later. Once you have a good sigil drawn on parchment, then, prior to using it, you can perform the rite to consecrate the sigil. You can also keep a sigil without consecrating it, and it will remain inactive until you charge and sacralize it. Once it has been consecrated and used in a ritual, you might keep it in a magical book or in a folder with other sigils.

Keep in mind that a sigil is just the first step in getting the symbolic identification for a spirit. You will need a sigil of a spirit's name to perform a conjuration, but once you have successfully conjured a spirit, then you can retrieve further marks of identification from them. The most powerful symbol of a spirit that you can construct and consecrate is a magical seal, but just a mark or symbol shown to you by the spirit will suffice as well. As long as the spirit recognizes its own mark, then it can be used to summon or call a spirit without any ritual workings. The sigil is the calling card, but the mark, signature, or seal is the actual material link to that spirit. However, like the sigil, the mark, signature, or seal must be fully consecrated and shown to the spirit before it can be used to summon that entity at any time.

One single point I would like to make is that when you summon a spirit, it isn't like calling a friend and then having them come over to visit you. In the material world, when a person travels to see someone, they aren't anywhere else other than where they are. A spirit is more like an animated and disembodied symbolic being. They are real to the conscious senses of the magician, but they don't actually occupy any space or time, and they can be in more than one location at a time.

What that means is that you aren't getting the one and only version of that spirit when you summon it, and, in fact, hundreds or even thousands of individual magicians could be summoning the same spirit and get a full and complete experience from the event without duplication, omission, delay, or a diminished manifestation. Spirits are ubiquitous and without material bodies, so they obey a completely different set of rules other than those constraining the material world. When you summon a spirit, you won't get a busy signal or an answering service saying that the entity is currently unavailable.

The spirit's name, translated into a sigil, acts as the first step to summoning them. Acquiring additional identification is the whole purpose of summoning them, aside from any pact or task that you would have them to assist you in achieving. Using an alphabet wheel to build a sigil will be the core activity for any conjuration, and as you can see, it is a simple and efficient task. It is also quite effective. I have used this technique for decades with the greatest success.

We will discuss the topic of seals and how to construct them in greater detail, but that task requires that you successfully conjure spirits and make full contact with them first. Acquiring a mark or signature is a good outcome for an invocation or evocation, and it can suffice for any magical working that requires a special relationship forged between the magician and spirit.

CHAPTER THREE

BRIEF DISCUSSION ABOUT ANGELIC AND DEMONIC SEALS

Perhaps the most influential and notable representatives of a spirit are the various marks and signatures that are called *magical seals*. They can be quite elaborate, as in the seals of the seventy-two Goetic demons or the various seals of the *Grimoire Armadel*, or quite crude, as some of the seals and marks of the demon spirits from the *Grimoirum Verum* and other lesser-known grimoires. Suffice it to say that these seals were constructed and invented by someone at some point in time, and in some cases, like the seals for the Goetic demons, enhanced and embellished by many individuals before becoming the famous representations they are presently.

Since these spirit tokens are believed to be the veritable signatures of the spirits themselves, few have investigated or determined the author or the historical evolution of these graphic images. That task will have to be performed by an accredited historian familiar with these graphic anomalies; until that time, we can only assume their authorship and origins.

What I can say about magical seals is that they were invented by individuals in collusion with the spirits themselves, and that they represent a graphic representation that a spirit will acknowledge as an authorized signature and calling card. It can be said, then, that the seal represents the symbolic essence of a spirit. When it is drawn on parchment or etched on a metallic medallion, charged, and consecrated, it functions as a doorway between that spirit and the magician.

Once a spirit has been conjured, if its seal is already a known part of a specific magical grimoire or tradition and it has been charged and consecrated, the magician may wield the seal as a magical tool that allows them to directly summon the spirit to assist with some objective. There are quite a few sets of magical seals that a magician can acquire, construct, and use in their conjuration tasks. Having such a seal allows them to wield the powers and authority of that spirit. Still, in some cases, there won't be a traditional seal that the magician can construct. In those situations, the magician may construct their own seal after consultation with a spirit that has been fully conjured. Keeping in mind that someone at some point in time had to have created the seals that are part of various traditions of magic today, it is completely acceptable for a magician to fashion a seal for a spirit that doesn't have one.

In this chapter, we will cover the spectrum of seals, signatures, and marks available to a practicing magician and where they can be found; examine some of them to note how they are constructed; and discuss how to construct magical seals for spirits who do not have them. The approach to constructing your own magical seals can be simple or elaborate; however, it is always a collaborative effort between you and the spirit that you conjured. This is, then, a truly creative process, and you will use your graphic skills and imagination, along with a consultation with the target spirit, to produce a magical seal that will facilitate summoning and embodying the powers and authority of that spirit into the moment's magical objective.

DEMONIC SEALS

The most famous spirit seals can be found in the *Lemegeton*, or the *Lesser Key of Solomon*, in the first book of that series known as the *Goetia (Ars Goetia)*. While the spirit list was being handed around in the mid to late sixteenth century, the seals didn't appear until around the seventeenth century, when the *Lemegeton* was assembled. In the earlier spirit list likely assembled by Agrippa but made public by his student, Johann Weyer, in his book *Pseudomonarchia Daemonum*, there weren't the seventy-two spirits known later in the *Goetia* included in that list. There were only a select number of around sixty-eight spirits, and there were no seals accompanying those demons.[10] At some point, someone obviously developed the famous Goetic seals, and they became an integral part of the *Goetia* grimoire. Some have speculated that that perhaps Johanne Trithemius might have developed these seals, but since they don't appear in any manuscripts until the seventeenth century, it makes this occurrence unlikely.

Looking over the seventy-two seals of the Goetic spirits, one can see a lot of fabulous variations, where it seems that the makers of these seals used parts of letters, crosses, spirals, squiggles, parts of planetary symbols, vulgar graffiti, and various suggestive animal shapes that may or may not be based on the qualities of the spirits themselves. Each are enclosed by a circle, perhaps to contain or constrain them in some manner. Some occultists have seen a system or pattern in the structure of these seals and believe that important information is somehow embedded in them. I have found that this kind of speculation is prone to hubris and cannot either determine the thoughts and impressions behind the author of these seals nor their collaboration with the spirits themselves.

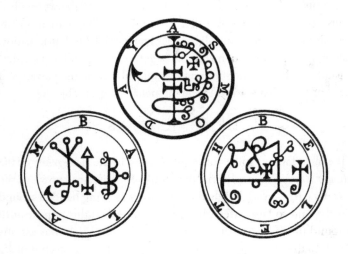

---

10 Peterson, Joseph H., *The Lesser Key of Solomon* (Weiser Books, 2001) p. xiii–xiv.

What can be seen in examining these seals is a very complex and unique graphic artform that seeks to capture the essence of the demonic spirit, and I believe that this objective is quite successful. Each seal is unique yet related to the others in the set. It is obvious from looking at them that a very sophisticated hand has been at work, and these seals have an inherent esthetic value that is doubtlessly why they continue to capture the imagination of occultists and magicians to this day.

I think that we can leave the whole deciphering approach of the Goetic seals to those with too much time on their hands and just accept that they are a part of the tradition of the system of the Goetic demons. Therefore, if you want to evoke one of these spirits to establish a relationship with them, the use of the consecrated seal is an important part of that process. Instead of trying to figure out what each of these seals is attempting to communicate, we can accept them as they are in that tradition and either use them or not, depending on the objectives and methods of our magic.

In that same book series of the *Lemegeton*, the *Theurgia Goetia* also has seals for the Emperors, Grand Dukes, Dukes, and Princes of that traditional system. They are similar to the Goetic seals, but of a much simpler design. It is likely that these seals may not have been as popularly known as the Goetic seals, and so they are not as embellished and refined.[11]

---

11 See Skinner, Stephen and David Rankine, *The Goetia of Dr. Rudd* (Llewellyn Publications, 2010) pp. 218–307 for the entire chapter on the *Theurgia Goetia*, the magical seals, and the spirits and their qualities.

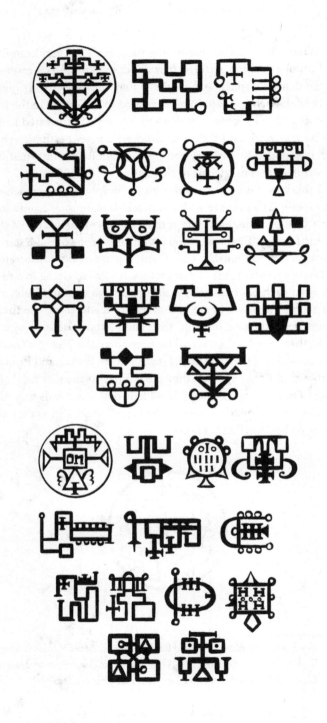

The *Grimoirum Verum,* probably one of the most notorious grimoires in history, also makes use of seals for the various demons, although they appear to be simpler or cruder than what is depicted in the *Goetia.* The grimoire refers to these seals as "characters," but they are recognizable as similar in construction and function as to those seals in the *Goetia,* so we can consider them as seals for our purposes. The seals for the three demonic chiefs, which are Lucifer, Beelzebub, and Astaroth, are more elaborate than the seals for other demons.[12]

Seals of Lucifer from the Grimorium Verum

---

12 See Stratton-Kent, Jake, *The True Grimoire* (Scarlet Imprint, 2022) pp. 60–78 to examine the full set of seals associated with the *Grimoirum Verum.*

The seals from the demon lists can consist of different figures grouped together or by a simple linear structure, but overall, the demonic seals are simple and less elaborate than their cousins in the *Goetia*.

Seals of Bucon and Sogal from the Grimorium Verum

As we examine seals that are shown in other grimoires, such as the *Grand Grimoire* or the *Grimoire of Pope Honorius*, we can see a variety of structures employed. Some are elaborate and some simple, but none of them are as elaborate as the seals of the *Goetia*. If you are working through a specific grimoire, you would employ those seals as they are depicted in a manner that corresponds to the text of that magical book. Keep in mind, whether or not the grimoire states that the characters or seals have to be consecrated, you should assume that in order to activate them, you would have to consecrate and charge them in a ritual.

If a grimoire already describes the characters and seals representing the various demonic spirits, then it is assumed that the magician will use them in their work. It is important to consider the power and authority of a seal that has been used for centuries as opposed to designing and constructing a seal that already exists. My recommendation is that you design and employ a seal for spirits that do not have such a representation, but you should use those that are already defined.

ANGELIC SEALS

Angels have seals as well, although they are not typically as famous and well-known as the seals for Goetic demons. They can be found in many places, including books and even the internet. However, by examining these seals, one can see that they tend to be linear, balanced, and without any of the more wild and vulgar representations that we find when examining the Goetic seals. Perfect examples of the seals of the archangels can be found in the book *Grimoire Armadel*, which was discovered in the Arsenal Library in Paris and translated and published by S. L. MacGregor Mathers.[13] Other seals can be found for the seventy-two Ha-Shem angels, but beyond the most famous angels, the rest are unrepresented.

There are other representations of the seals of archangels, and these can also be found in various source books and online. These seals are much simpler and consist typically of a linear structure incorporating lines, triangles, crosses, curlicues, and

---

13 See Mathers, S. L. MacGregor, *The Grimoire of Armadel*, (Samuel Weiser Inc, 1980) edited by Francis King, pp. 23–67 for examples of the sigils and seals of the angel and demons, especially the seven planetary archangels.

other uncomplicated structures that seem to be made from a single flowing line, much like a sigil. The exception is the seal of Haniel, the archangel of Venus, where one of the figures in the seal resembles an erect phallus.[14]

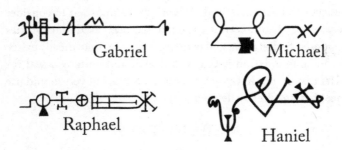

Seals of the archangels, as depicted in the *Grimoire Armadel*, are enclosed by two concentric circles forming an outer ring that is decorated with holy and magical names of God separated by crosses. They are quite elegant and detailed, obviously having been worked on by many individuals over time. Since the *Grimoire Armadel* is likely from the late seventeenth or early eighteenth century, then these seals have probably been around for several decades, passed around by occultists ever since Mathers discovered and published them in the early twentieth century.

Not much is known about the *Grimoire Armadel*, since no other versions have been found so far, and the copy that we have in the Arsenal Library in Paris is probably an incomplete and corrupted version of the original. However, the angelic seals have made this book famous, and the numerous other seals and characters found within it are quite beautifully drawn and pleasing to the eye of magicians.

---

14 Mathers, S. L. MacGregor, *The Grimoire of Armadel* (Samuel Weiser Inc, 1980) edited by Francis King, p. 43.

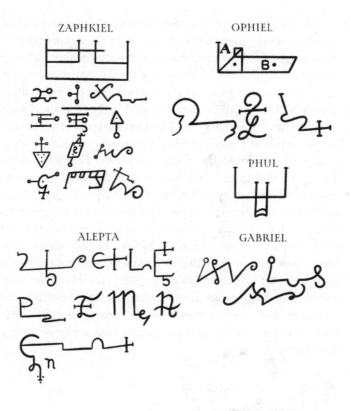

Often, the seven planetary archangels are associated with the seals of the seven Olympian spirits as developed by students of Paracelsus and found in the grimoire *Arbatel*.[15] These seals are simple linear designs that do not have any curves in their design, representing straightforward structures that are impressive in their simplicity. While these seven Olympian spirits are a separate class of entities, representing the qualities of the seven planetary intelligences, they could be equated with the seven planetary archangels. This is often the case in popular graphic representations.

---

15   Peterson, Joseph H., *Arbatel: Concerning the Magic of the Ancients* (Ibis Press, 2009) pp. 32–39.

I have worked extensively with the Olympian spirits and have found them to be particularly efficacious. In the various grimoires, there are representations of the seals of the planetary archangels that are not associated with the seals of the Olympian spirits, so it is likely that combining them may not actually represent a traditional approach, although this process is found in the *Grimoire Armadel*.

Seals for the seventy-two Ha-Shem angels, as I call them, or the angels of the Shem Ha-Mephorash, are more obscure, although I have found them online in a few different locations.[16] The reason that these angels have seals is that they were used to counter the seventy-two demons of the *Goetia*, so pairing them in this manner gives the operator greater control and protection from the demonic spirits. While this does appear in the Goetia of Dr. Rudd and is mentioned in Sibley's *Key of Solomon*, it was likely a practical consideration for producing seals for these angels (although that is speculation on my part). The Ha-Shem angels and the process to invoke them represent a magical discipline that is set apart from the evocation of Goetic demons, and these angels have their own powers and authorities that are quite separate from demonic magic.

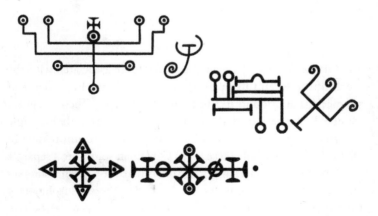

---

16 "Search for 'angels of the Shem Ha-Mephorash' on Adobe Stock Pictures" (paywall enforced), March 27, 2024, https://stock.adobe.com

Beyond the archangels and Ha-Shem angels, magical seals are omitted for the rest of the massive hosts of angelic spirits. Even the Seraphim and Cherubim have no seals that I have been able to find, so I had to use sigils and an elaborate invocation rite to summon them. This is either due to the fact that many angels are not as popular as demons, except for those that are pre-eminent in the various magical traditions, or that the magician does not need to employ a seal to establish a relationship with them. My experience with angelic beings is that they respond quite well when I use a simple sigil to invoke them, so perhaps this is why only the famous ones have seals.

Needless to say, as creative magicians, we have the option to construct our own seals whenever we find a need to do so.

CONSTRUCTING MAGICAL SEALS

Before attempting to construct a magical seal, it would be a good idea to examine a number of examples, whether of demons or angels, to get a clue what the seal that you want to construct might look like. You might also want to determine if the spirit would be classified as angelic, demonic, or neutral. There are variations in style based on the class of spirit that would be depicted by a seal, but what you produce doesn't necessarily need to fit this model approach. We have discussed that angelic seals appear to be linear and harmonious, and demonic seals tend to contain curves, circles, and squiggles, and are more dramatic and outrageous.

Creating a seal has two basic stages. The first stage is to draw the seal in a direct and impulsive manner after communing with the spirit, and the second stage is to refine and embellish that drawing once it is committed to paper. You can skip the second stage if you feel that what you have produced in the initial stage is sufficient or if you want to keep the raw and spontaneous image intact without refining it. Whatever you decide to do will depend on the initial outcome and whether it fits your esthetic expectations. Additionally, the final product must be agreeable to the spirit that it represents so it can be used as a summoning device.

As I have previously stated, constructing a seal occurs under the guidance of the spirit that has already been conjured. If you have successfully conjured a spirit using a sigil representing its name, then you can commune with that spirit through the consecrated sigil and, with its aid, design a seal that is a suitable signature for that entity.

Here are a set of steps that I follow to construct a magic seal. It is a simple working performed to produce a seal of an already conjured spirit. It is important to perform this kind of activity in a sacred space, so performing the rite to consecrate a circle is an important first step. Take a pad of paper with pencils, pen, or a Magic Marker with you to draw the seal. You can refine it later using your drafting tools, but to get the basic seal, it is a good idea to make it as simple and direct as possible.

1. Sit in the middle of a consecrated magic circle with writing implements and a pad of paper. Bring the consecrated sigil of the spirit with you.
2. Enter into a light trance state and, while holding the sigil, call the spirit to appear to your mind's eye.
3. When the spirit appears or is sensible in some manner, put down the sigil and take up the paper and pen, then request that the spirit show you its mark or seal.
4. Draw what the spirit shows to you. This might appear as more than one image, so draw each one as you see it in your mind's eye. (This is why you have a pad of paper instead of just one piece.)
5. Coalesce the drawings into a single set of images on one piece of paper, if there is more than one image, and present it to the spirit, asking it to affirm the design or to show any other images or adjustments to the design to complete it. Continue with this effort until the spirit affirms that the image presented is correct and complete.
6. Once this is done, make an offering of incense and any other substance that would be pleasing to the spirit (drink, food, or both) and thank it for the help rendered.

7. Announce that this completed raw form symbolizes the spirit, and that variations of it can be used to summon that spirit whenever required.
8. Thank the spirit for appearing and give it the license to depart.
9. End the working in the traditional manner (banishment or sealing).

Once you have the raw design of the seal, you can decide to refine it and embellish it using your drafting tools. You might decide not to alter it and keep it the way it was initially conceived. That will be your choice, of course.

Take the completed design and draw it on a piece of parchment. You could also etch it on a metallic disk or even use enameling or paint to produce a more permanent representation. The final product is then charged and consecrated, thereby making it fully activated. Keep it in a cloth pouch and take it out and use only when needed.

When summoning the spirit with the seal, hold it in your hand and call the spirit in your mind several times until you sense its appearance, then give it a purpose or objective and send it to perform that task. You should determine the approximate time or date when you would expect that task to be completed. Of course, your request should be in alignment with the spirit and its capabilities, and the time allotted should be reasonable. You might also want to consider the lunar, solar, and planetary auspices if the request is for something important or strategic, since these might have an influence on the successful outcome of the request.

I need to provide an example of how you can construct a seal. I had been working with a group of spirits known as the fallen angels of the Nephilim, and although they were quite known in Hebrew folklore and have Hebrew spellings, there are no traditional seals associated with them. The exception is Azazel, whose seal looks a lot like the planetary seal for Saturn. However, the rest of the twenty chiefs of the Nephilim were not represented with a seal.

Because I needed to create seals for nineteen of these spirits (except Azazel), I used the above technique to contact them, and one by one, over a period of an hour, I successfully was shown their seals. I used a composition notebook that has writing guidelines to get these seals, and then once that was done, I transferred the designs to a circle format for each seal.

Here is an example of what the seal of Shemichaz looked like as a raw seal received directly from that spirit:

And here is an example of what the seal of Shemichaz looked like after I transferred the design to circle and refined it. I didn't change much to the initial raw design, but once transferred to a circle, it was made ready to be made into a parchment seal that I could consecrate.

CHAPTER FOUR

CONDENSING LETTER FORMS INTO MAGICAL SIGNATURES

If you want to create a magical seal without first having to invoke or evoke a spirit, so you can have the seal on hand when you first perform the conjuration, then there is a quick and dirty way to do this by making sigils of aspiration to construct a magical signature or character. While this method will not produce the ornate and engaging magical seal that is the hallmark of a collaborative effort between the spirit and the magician, it can be used to get something on parchment in addition to the sigil to reinforce the techniques of spirit conjuration. You can use this approach if the spirit is neutral or angelic, but if you want a mark or signature for any kind of demon that has no seal, then I would recommend using the technique of constructing a seal as previously shown in Chapter Three. That being said, I leave the decision regarding how to proceed with you, the reader and magical operator.

Since we have covered a sigil that is derived from an alphabet wheel and its linear design, another kind of sigil used in magic consists of a process of reducing, condensing, and restructuring the letters of the name of spirit using the English alphabet. You could also perform this operation using the Hebrew or Greek alphabet, or any other alphabet since the steps are applied to the letters of the name in whatever form they might appear. We will look at this methodology in a more detailed manner in Part III of this book, but for now, we will use this technique to create a character, mark, or signature based on the letters of a spirit's name.

CONSTRUCTING A SPIRIT'S MARK OR MAGICAL SIGNATURE

The method of crafting a magical signature has three basic steps and is simpler than crafting a sigil based on an objective or aspiration, as we shall see in Part III. The purpose here is to reduce and condense the forms to create a single graphic representation from the name of the spirit.

1. Eliminate duplicate letters in the name so that each letter is only represented once. Let's say that we want to create a signature of the demon Azazel, who has a seal, but we want something that doesn't look like the seal for the planetary seal of Saturn. So, if we eliminate the duplicate letters for AZAZEL, we will have the four letters A Z E L.
2. Eliminate the letters that are variations of the same shape. If we look at the four letters and break out the common shapes so that they appear only once, then we will have a left and right slanting line, a straight horizontal line, and a straight vertical line. These are the four shapes that we have reduced the name down to build our mark.
3. Take the reduced list of shapes and reassemble them into a unique graphic representation that graphically represents the spirit's qualities. Once you have a form that looks esthetically pleasing, you can embellish and refine it until you are completely satisfied with the results.

What I have found while following these three simple steps is that the final reassembly may require some experimentation before the right graphic representation is found. Some names have more complex letter structures, such as an "O," which can be kept intact but reduced in size, and of course letters with curves, such as a "B," "D," "S," "C," "G," "J," "P," "U," or "Q," would be broken up into separate and opposing curves, and the lines would be subsumed into the vertical or horizontal lines of the other letters. We chose a simple name to show how it can be done, but there is much artistry in reducing a name down into a sigil-like graphical representation.

Here is an example of the steps that I followed to produce a signature for Azazel:

I should also include a more complex example. Here are the steps that I followed to produce a signature for Lucifuge. In any situation, you will follow the three steps to condense, break down into the letter forms, and then reassemble them to formulate a new graphical representation of the spirit's name.

Using this technique, you will never be without some kind of seal or signature for a specific spirit before actually going through the process of performing the invocation or evocation. When writing this book, I felt that it was important to give you a number of approaches to building a symbolic link to aid in your efforts to perform a conjuration. My purpose was to show a variety of techniques and approaches so that you might not be locked into a single approach or lack the ability to even perform this task. Since creativity and imagination are important tools in building a seal or signature, more options presented by me may inspire you to develop other methods that are completely outside of this tradition.

USING THE TAROT TO DEFINE A SPIRIT'S QUALITIES

The Shakespearean quote from *Romeo and Juliet* states, "What's in a name?" In the art of spirit conjuration, we would have to ironically reply, "*everything!*" A spirit's name is the true measure of its meaning and essential qualities, similar in fashion to a person's name and identity. However, a spirit, which is disembodied and typically conforms to the image or formulation that the magician has within their imagination, has only its name to fully represent itself.

Many magicians and occultists have sought to tease out of a traditional spirit's name some kind of in a semantic meaning. We know that often first names have a meaning in another language, but a first name is almost always joined to a surname and even a middle name to fully identify a person. Some cultures also add the father's name or mother's name, or another family name to a person's list of names used to identify them with a family and a society. Teasing meaning out of a last name can be tricky, but not impossible. However, it can be quite difficult to tease the meaning out of the name of a spirit, and even so, what we have is the associated folklore and beliefs over time to support those meanings.

For instance, the demon's name Lucifer means "light-bearer," which hardly matches all of the folklore and occult characterizations, as well as the Goetic magical tradition. The name Beelzebub means "Lord of the Flies," which would imply a demon of stenches, defecation, and putrefaction, positive attracters for flies and other pestilence. He is listed in occult lore as one of the seven demon princes of Hell and presides over the sins of gluttony and envy.

However, some linguists, such as I, have noted that the name Beelzebub is a corruption of Baal Zebul (Lord of the Sky), which would be one of the primary names of the god Bel (also Bel-Hadad), one of the chief competitors of the Hebrew deity Yahweh, and means "Lord of Heaven." A simple trick of language changes the name from a Canaanite storm god to the pejorative name of a stinky demon. I could go on and on with this analysis, but ultimately it serves little purpose. The occult lore and Goetic tradition appears to have the final word on the matter. Lesser-known spirit names and entities, especially the names of local spirits, would likely be more difficult to trace and have a lot less lore to define them.

If only there were a way to take the name of a spirit and determine what that name means without having to play linguistic games or tease out the meaning based on the language used to derive that name. I came up with such a technique that I have used over the decades, and it appears to work quite well. That technique takes the letters of the spirit's name and associates them with the Trumps of the Major Arcana of the Tarot, and then, with the cards selected, I will perform a tarot card reading to get at the essence of that name.

Of course, the one issue that can make this association a little tough is that we would need to associate the letters of a spirit's name, which could be in any language, to the twenty-two letters of the Hebrew alphabet, which is the association of letters to the Trump cards in the Tarot. We have already encountered this problem when examining the art of letter substitution for magical squares, but we can remedy this by expanding the use of twenty-two letters so that they can include vowels used in other alphabets.

Here is how I would make the association between the twenty-two Trumps of the Tarot with the twenty-two letters, expanded to include letters and vowels for English. This should cover the need to substitute a letter in whatever language with a Tarot card.

Letter	Tarot Trump Card	Trump Card Meaning
A	0: The Fool	Meditation, caution, refusal of the call
B	I: Magus/Magician	Apotheosis
G	II: Priestess	Supernatural intervention
D	III: Empress	Foundation, golden age
H, E	XVII: The Star	Primal emanations
V, U, W	V: The Hierophant	Mastery of two worlds
Z medial, end	VI: The Lovers	Sacred marriage, union of light and darkness
Ch, C, X	VII: The Chariot	Ecstasy as method, obtaining the grail
T medial, end	XI: Lust/Strength	Inner strength, source of power, discipline
Y, I, J	IX: The Hermit	Guardian of the threshold, lintel crossing
K	X: The Wheel of Fortune	Mastery of death, overcoming the trials
L	VIII: Balance/Justice	Internal illumination, refusal of the return

Condensing Letter Forms into Magical Signatures

Letter	Tarot Trump Card	Trump Card Meaning
M	XII: The Hanged Man	Spiritual transformation, final dissolution
N	XIII: Death	Metamorphosis, catharsis, age of disease and death
S	XIV: Art/Temperance	Alchemy, great work (vision communication)
P, F	XVI: The Tower	Underworld, belly of the whale, domain of inner trials
A'in, O	XV: The Devil	Initiation, atonement with the dark father
Tz, Z initial	IV: The Emperor	Healing of the fisher king, rescue from without
Q	XVIII: The Moon	Mythic flight from the underworld, the return
R	XIX: The Sun	Freedom to live, achievement of hero's journey
Sh	XX: The Aion/Last Judgement	The call to adventure, awakening
Th, initial T	XXI: The Universe/World	The collective source, beginning and end

As you can see from this table, I have grouped letters together where they make the most sense in association with the Hebrew alphabet, and this should cover a spirit's name letters if they are in Hebrew or some approximation of Latin or English. Some of these expanded letter categories would be obvious, some not so much. For instance, there is no Ain in English, but it could be replaced with an O, and this substitution can be found in use by other occultists, such as Israel Regardie. You might need to add some additional letters if you are working with other alphabets, but what I have presented here should accommodate most of the spirit names that you might want to translate into a Tarot card reading using just the Trump cards. You should also note that I use both Crowley's Tarot Trump name as well as the traditional names, and I have switched the letters associated with The Star and The Emperor, since I do find what Crowley determined for these letters works for me. The card meanings are taken from the seventeen stages of Joseph Campbell's Hero's Journey and the five stages of the Cosmogonic Cycle, but you can use whatever card meanings work for you.

While I may have combined letters that only vaguely fit the structure of the twenty-two letters of the Hebrew alphabet, you might be wondering if this method confounds my promoting the use of alphabet wheels so that this kind of sloppy derivation can be avoided. If that is the case, then proposing the same sort of thing when associating letters to Tarot cards could be construed as contradictory. I suppose that it is, but here we are going about the process of selecting Tarot cards to do a reading in this instance, and in the other instance, we are crafting a sigil, so I do believe that the first can be an approximation and the second should be more exact. That, of course, is just my opinion, but I don't think that it negates this method of extracting additional meaning from the name of a spirit. We should try a wide range of possible techniques to find what works best—and what doesn't work very well—and then choose the most useful approach.

Now, on to the business of deriving the meaning of a spirit's name by the associated Tarot cards and examining them as if they were a card reading using just the Trump cards. Let's look at an example and see what kind of reading we will get.

So, the demon prince named LUCIFER would pull the following Tarot Trump cards:

1. VIII: Balance
2. V: The Hierophant
3. VII: The Chariot
4. IX: The Hermit
5. XVI: The Tower
6. XVII: The Star
7. XIX: The Sun

This is how I would interpret the meaning of the Tarot cards, and of course, you could get a different interpretation out of the same cards compared to what I came up with. The objective of the reading is to look at the cards as if you were using them to do a reading on a person to obtain information about their character.

> *Lucifer: This spirit has great virtues and was a powerful angel that kept the balance of light and darkness, travelled between worlds, and administered the divine grace and blessings to all living things (spiritual grail holder). However, he was a strident idealist who had tendencies toward aloofness and secretiveness, but it was his pride and belief in his own invincibility that caused his downfall. Still, because he was instrumental in the creation of the universe, he has been accorded certain freedoms and has kept his power and authority, even though he is divorced from the Deity and no longer in alignment with the Divine Will and Purpose.*

That sounds pretty interesting and does give us a lot more information than what is to be found in traditional characterizations. It is, in fact, a kind of intimate snapshot of the fallen angel called Lucifer. Based on this reading, you would know that to conjure this demon it would be prudent to treat him with a great deal of respect and reverence. He might be a fallen angel, but he still has a lot of power, ability, and wisdom to dispense if one were to approach him with the dignity and respect that he would require. Neglecting this approach would produce undesirable consequences unless one were ready to deal with an angry and very hostile demon, which would certainly thwart the intentions for performing the conjuration in the first place. In this situation, the more information you have, the better the outcome. Knowledge is power.

You can use this approach to get an intimate characterization of a spirit and realize what kind of character and temperament that entity has before you decide to perform a conjuration. This approach will work against any spirit name and is particularly useful to help you determine the nature and character of a spirit that has little or no lore. As I said, I have used this method for many decades, and it has always proved to be both useful and insightful. Through the use of this method, you will never blindly invoke or evoke a spirit without a more thorough understanding of their nature and their character. It will help you better prepare for a conjuration rite, and that might make the difference between a bad experience and a good and productive one.

I would like to add that my book *Spirit Conjuring for Witches* has an extensive amount of material written about invoking or evoking spirits and the means and methods for constructing sigil and communicating with spirits. I recommend this book if you are interested in examining these techniques in greater detail.

PART II

ALPHABET OF ASPIRATIONS: SIGILS, WORDS, AND PHRASES OF POWER

CHAPTER FIVE

METHOD OF SIGIL CREATION FROM WORDS AND PHRASES

Now that we have examined the various techniques associated with spirit names and how those tasks can greatly assist the art of conjuration, there is another whole category of sigils that should be examined. These are sigils that are derived from phrases that describe desires, aspirations, and magical objectives.

This kind of sigil creation is a much later development, and it was developed by an occultist and magician named Austin Osman Spare, who lived in England during the last decades of the nineteenth century into the middle of the twentieth century. He was an obscure individual who was a phenomenal graphic artist, illustrator, magician, and cunning man. Since he was such an iconoclast and social outcast, he lived the life of a recluse with little income and without much notice in the art world of his time.

We would probably not know anything about him or his magical graphic techniques had it not been for the popular occultist, Thelemic magician, and author named Kenneth Grant. Grant wrote extensively about him, discussed his magical methods, and popularized his artwork. Suffice it to say, I won't include any biographical notes about Spare and his life since that is covered by other authors and their work, but I will discuss the magical graphic methods that he used to forge his art and his magic in this chapter, since both were intertwined.

Spare's graphical methods were immediately adopted by the nascent tradition of Chaos magicians after Grant's popularized the techniques, but others found it useful as well. Perhaps the best work available on Spare's magical methods is to be found in the book *Practical Sigil Magic* authored by Frater U. D.[17] I highly recommend this work to you as an adjunct to my book. Frater U. D. goes deeper into a lot of the details and techniques that Spare developed, so, if you want to know much more than what I have in this chapter, then you can read his book.

In this chapter, I will cover how to craft sigils of aspiration and examine the ancillary methods and techniques that are used to build sigils that can function as a magical link between one's desires and aspirations and the symbolic representation of that objective. Creating an empowered magical link can be useful in working with the advanced energy model constructions that I have advocated for in my writings, and they can also be used by themselves to project magical powers and bend the probabilities that separates a potential desire from actual material realization. I believe that harnessing this technique is a critical part of performing magical operations that are successful and materially realized.

In addition to sigils of aspiration, I will also briefly cover the art of pictograms, words of power, Spare's alphabet of desire, magical alphabets, magical formulas, and the art of magical notaries. We will examine the techniques, methods, and directives for translating magical objectives into powerful symbolic representations, understanding that the sigil acts as a link or bridge between the subject and the target. What is needed to activate them is to supply the magical energy, and the spell is, more or less, complete. Let us begin this approach with a simplified version of Spare's techniques of crafting sigils from sentences or phrases so that our aspirations might become symbolic links to materialized realization.

---

17 Frater U. D., Practical Sigil Magic: Creating Personal Symbols of Success (Llewellyn Publications, 1990).

Method of Sigil Creation from Words and Phrases

We have already used a simple version of reducing, condensing, and restructuring the letters in a spirit's name to produce a signature or mark of that spirit. To capture the graphical representation of a phrase requires a couple more steps and some basic considerations. Let us proceed with the business of learning how to fashion a sigil from a phrase.

The first thing that we need to note is that the affirmation or objective that we are seeking should be written down. It should be strongly worded, positive, and include some degree of passion or emphasis. Avoid using the words "might," "should," or "could," and definitely avoid using the negative quality, as in "not something." What you write should always be declarative, clearly stated, and direct. Weak statements or vague pronouncements will fail to produce the results that you are seeking.

When you want something from the spirit world or to manifest something in the material world, it is best not to beat around the bush. Politeness, decorum, and good manners are irrelevant and, in fact, may cloud or muddy your objective. Your target needs to be clearly and efficiently stated in order to be truly realized in a magical format. Also, eliminate unnecessary verbiage from your sentence, so the terms "I desire" or "I want" are good candidates for elimination. This is an aspiration, so the idea of *desire* or *want* should be implicit. The first word should indicate what it is that you want or desire.

Suppose that you are single and without any lover at the moment, and you would like to change that situation so that you could have someone to be a partner to you and also engage in sex together. You would want to carefully articulate exactly what you are seeking. Are you seeking someone to build a real lasting relationship, or do you just want someone to sexualize or to socialize? Clarifying exactly what you intend to do is quite important if you expect a specific outcome. While you could specifically target an actual person, in my example I will keep the options for a relationship open and focus the objective on finding a lasting relationship without naming someone. While my example might be ethical, what you might get up to is completely your own business.

In clarifying your search for a lasting relationship, it would also be prudent to state the physical conditions or mental health of the person who might fit with your objective. You may want to avoid a person who has mental health concerns, is unable to have a relationship (isn't single or in an open partnership), or doesn't fit with your sense of esthetics. You want to avoid using negatives in your aspiration, so you might phrase what you are seeking in the following manner.

First, what are you seeking?

Seeking a long-term relationship.

Let's assume that a long-term relationship is a bond like marriage.

What are your requirements? Here is where you will qualify what you are looking for in a relationship. Let's assume that you are a heterosexual male, but of course, your search could be for any kind of relationship with any gender depending on your sexual preferences and identity. This might then be defined as:

Single, attractive, healthy, good-natured, woman, like interests.

You could add other qualities, but this should be sufficient to define someone for a heterosexual male who is seeking to have a healthy long-term relationship with a woman. The whole phrase would be:

Seeking marriage with single, attractive, healthy, good-natured, woman with like interests.

That should allow for a number of possibilities, but with the parameters defined, the outcome would not likely be disappointing. Now that we have gotten the phrase established, we can remove the words "with" and "seeking" since they are implied in the aspiration. We can also replace "good-natured" with the word "good," and the phrase "like interests" with the word "same."

The phrase would look like this:

Marriage, single, attractive, healthy, good, woman, same.

The first thing that we will do to this perfect phrase of aspiration is to make the letters capitalized and then remove the redundant letters so that each letter only appears once. This is the reduction process. Our phrase would look like this set of letters:

MARIGESNLTCVHYOW

We could also break it into two sets of letters by isolating the word "woman" so that it has precedence, because only the "W" for the word "woman" is used in the reduced phrase. We will then remove the "W" from the first string and make a new letter string from just the word "woman," so we would have a first and second string that looked like this.

MARIGESNLTCVHYO

WOMAN

Using the reduction for these two strings of letters, we can begin the breaking out of the forms of the letters and then reconstructing them into a new graphic form. I was able to condense the first string into seven different shapes, and the second string into five shapes.

Here is an example of what those different shapes would look like:

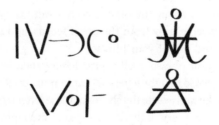

Then, I will take those condensed shapes and formulate a graphical representation. I can slightly embellish them so that they are somewhat recognizable, but I have faithfully used the basic shapes to creatively fashion two sigils: one represents the intention and the second, the objective.

This is an example of what those two finished sigils would look like:

The results of this process will produce sigils that symbolically represent the aspiration of seeking and finding a long-term relationship. Of course, the sigil by itself, even after being charged and consecrated, requires corresponding mundane steps to ensure that one would be able to find opportunities to help bend and flex reality to produce the desired outcome.

Sigil construction then consists of five basic steps. These are the steps that you should follow when constructing a sigil that symbolically represents your magical objective based on a concise phrase or expression.

1. Build a sentence that concisely states your magical objective. Ensure that you have listed what you want as an outcome in a thorough manner. Eliminate extraneous words and focus on those that precisely list what you are seeking in an outcome. You may want to emphasize a word separately from the other words, and if so, take that word out of your phrase.
2. Write your phrase in all capital letters, then remove any duplicates so that the letters appear in your string only once.
3. Break out and isolate the shapes of those letters so that only the rudimentary unduplicated shapes are represented. If there are two or more strings of letters, do this to each set.

4. Use these shapes to construct a sigil or sigils, if there is more than one set of shapes, and represent them in the order that makes the most sense. Try multiple and different approaches to constructing a single graphic figure for each set of shapes.
5. Once the graphic sigils are fashioned, you can embellish them to make them look more esthetically pleasing.

Once you have determined the final design for the graphic sigil or sigils, draw them on a piece of parchment with a pen. You can use pencil to lightly trace the sigil form first, and then overlay that sketch with pen and ink. Now the sigil is ready to be consecrated and used.[18]

POWER OF PICTOGRAMS

We live in a world of pictograms—warning or danger signs, symbols, emoticons, traffic direction signs—and it would seem that the magical notary art also has symbolic images that can directly communicate meanings. This is, in fact, another facet of sigil magic. In the previous examples, we used words and phrases to create graphic symbols, but in this technique, we would either extend the graphic symbol into a pictogram, or we can start with an image and reduce and condense it down to a pictogram.

So, there are two different approaches to producing a pictogram sigil, and both of them are completely acceptable methodologies. A pictogram is a pictorial symbol for a word or phrase, and in fact, it is the source of most writing systems in the West. If you invert the letter "A," you will notice that it looks like a pictogram for the head of an ox, which, indeed, it is. All the letters of the alphabets that came from Proto-Canaanite letters were derived originally from pictograms. So, creating a pictogram from a word or phrase and making that into a magical emblem is actually a very modern preoccupation. Since the advance of the digital age, we

---

18 Frater U. D., *Practical Sigil Magic* (Llewellyn Publications, 1990) pp. 1–28. Two chapters outline Spare's methods for creating magical sigils to contrast what I have written.

have seen a prevalence of pictograms being used to communicate on public signs, streets and highways, and even social media. It would seem to be a devolution of the written language, except for the fact that images communicate more directly and quickly than written words. That is a known truth, and it should—and does—apply to the notary art of magic.

The first technique is to take the sigil produced in the four steps earlier and make final changes to it so that it resembles a pictogram more than a graphic sigil. Here is an example of what that would look like when applied to the sigil that we derived earlier.

Another approach is to use signs and stick figures, arrows, symbols, and the like to produce a pictogram from a series of graphic images or signs. This only requires two steps. The first is to take a phrase and make a series of simple images that denote its meaning, then the second step is to take that series of images and reduce them to a simpler combined graphic representation. We will use our example above and show how it would look by starting with images first and then reducing that to pictograms.

Pictogram of Proposal to Marry

As you can see, this is a simple task that requires a bit of artistry and imagination, but the end results are versatile and useful when incorporated into other forms of magic, most notably using the advanced energy model. Graphic images of any type facilitate the construction of magical links that are a critical part of most magical workings. The process of reducing a phrase or a series of pictographs down to a single graphic image forces you to also refine and reduce your magical design or purpose down to a manageable and clearly defined objective. If nothing else, simplifying and making an objective into a singular and passionate desire is one of the basic rules for achieving material success when working magic towards a goal.[19]

WORDS OF POWER, CHANTS, AND MANTRAS

Developing a graphic sigil is one of the ways to encapsulate a magical objective using a phrase or a sentence. However, this process of reduction can also be used to derive a chant, mantra, or set of words of power. If we use the reduction of redundant letters in a phrase, then we would also have a chant or mantra that we could use to impact the world of spirit through sound. This approach is probably more obscure and not intuitively obvious than others we've discussed. I would recommend that if you want to forge a graphical link, you can also derive a chant that you can use to give it power and emphasis, but I doubt that using such an approach by itself would be as efficacious or ubiquitous as a graphic image. (This is, of course, just my opinion.)

Taking the above reduced form for seeking a long-term relationship, we have a character string to work with in order to derive the chant:

MARIGESNLTCVHYOW

---

[19] Frater U. D., *Practical Sigil Magic* (Llewellyn Publications, 1990) pp. 43–52. This chapter outlines Spare's methodology for making pictograms for comparison.

This string is vowel-poor and therefore impossible to iteratively chant or memorize. There are four vowels—A, E, I, O—and the rest are consonants. You can rearrange the letters and group them with consonants, repeat vowels, and break the string into separate word-strings, so you might end up with a chant that looks like this:

Mariges Nolatich Veyow!

Without the graphic image, this might not convey quite as much meaning as it might combined with the sigil. However, another way of using this technique is to take expressions of power in your preferred language and command and condense them, which might make the whole process more interesting and esthetically pleasing.

Take this appellation and turn it into a word of power:

I am like the God of Fire commanding you to appear!

Turn this sentence into a string of letters:

*IAMLIKETHEGODOFFIRE
COMMANDINGYOUTOAPPEAR*

Remove any duplicates. This string of letters becomes like this reduced string:

IAMLKETHGODFRCNUTP

Then, this string could be made into the following chant:

Milketh Godic Frunatep!

This chanting expression of power might be nonsense to other magicians, but if you know its meaning and intent, it can become a chant of power. What I have produced above by the seat of my pants could be carefully refined and worked until it produces a phrase that has tremendous resonance and is easy to express and repeatedly chant. Using this technique can produce words of power that only have meaning to the magician expressing them and to anyone else who knows what the word actually means. Because the intent is so emotionally expressed in the words that have no meaning, they become words of power that have meaning within the domain of Spirit.

What I have learned in using traditional words of power and the Enochian language is that magical languages are based on the kind of sounds that they produce, and even if the meaning is lost, their intent is to raise the level of emotional energy and to emphatically express something that sounds foreign, strange, and arcane. Any intrinsic meaning is not as relevant as how they sound when recited and expressed by the magician.

Whether you develop your own words of power or use those words that come from a grimoire or are assembled from translated Enochian keys, what is produced is based on the expressive sounds of power that they produce. Of course, if a magician uses barbarous words of evocation in their magical workings, they should practice them often so that when they are reciting them in a ritual, they flow and seem like a natural language to the ears of the magician and whoever might be attending the rite.

However, I have known magicians who have used their native tongue and expressed themselves so powerfully and commandingly that embellishing that activity with another is unnecessary. This is a matter of esthetics, and whether you choose to use traditional words of power, derive your own words of power, or omit them entirely, has no bearing on the magic that is generated.[20]

SPARE'S ALPHABET OF DESIRE: A BRIEF OVERVIEW

One of the most interesting, and mostly indecipherable, elements of Spare's magical system is what he has called in his writings, the *alphabet of desire*. Although several authors have come up with their own interpretations of what this would entail, only

---

[20] Frater U. D., *Practical Sigil Magic* (Llewellyn Publications, 1990) pp. 55–61. This is the chapter that examines Spare's system of developing mantras and words of power.

Frater U. D. seems to have grasped what it means and how to deploy it in simple manner.[21] This was a popular trope amongst the founders of the chaos magic movement, but it was Kenneth Grant who expounded on it. Yet he also left out a lot of practical details that make it a useful system. Everyone, it seems, has their own theory and perspective on this technique, but it should be something straightforward and follow the basic rules for developing graphic sigils.

The main difference between producing an alphabet of desire as opposed to making sigils wherever or whenever needed is that it becomes a linguistic task to produce a suite of sigils that could potentially be used to define a magical objective. If you were to assemble of batch of sigils that represented all of the magical objectives that you might want to produce, and then added to that set some necessary ancillary concepts, such as your magical name, sigils for the terms "want," "seek," "receive," and maybe some sigil terms like "justice," "retribution," "money," "material success," and "fulfilled ambition," along with sigils for "love," "hate," "friendship," "truth," "deception," "insight," and other important words used in magical aspirations, then you would have an effective sigil language tool.

All you would need to do to build a sigil, then, would be to select ones from your set of already developed sigil concepts and use them to produce a sigil-based phrase or sentence that mirrors your magical objective. You would transcribe these sigils on a piece of parchment with pen and ink or inscribe them on a metal disk, and you would quickly have a powerful sigil to use in a magical working. The whole basis of this rather obscure and esoteric technique is to create a magical language based on sigils, and then assemble them to form sentences representing your magical objective.

This process can be as simple or complex as you want it to be, but having ready-made sigils developed from words and phrases

---

21 Frater U. D., *Practical Sigil Magic* (Llewellyn Publications, 1990) pp. 63–84. This chapter explores Spare's alphabet of desire, which is somewhat different than what I have proposed.

that are reuseable is the entire basis of this important and amazing magical technique. To create your own alphabet of aspirations, as I would call it, you should look over your many magical objectives and then pick out a set of words that you would likely use for any future magical workings. As time goes on, you might add new words to your set as you develop new objectives.

To develop a set of sigils for sigil sentence construction, you need to apply the same methodology to a single word that you would to a phrase. We did that earlier when we decided to have a separate sigil for the word "woman" in our long-term relationship aspiration sigil above.

The reduction phase of constructing a word-sigil eliminates duplicate letters, but in many situations, there might not be any duplicates, so start with the letters capitalized as a string and then perform the operation of breaking out the unduplicated shapes and reassembling them into a graphic sigil representation. You will perform this operation against each of the words in your magical vocabulary to create sigils and then keep them for any working that you might wish to perform.

The following steps will produce a sigil vocabulary that you can use an alphabet of aspirations:

1. Assemble a list of words that represent the kind of goals that you might use in any future magical working.
2. Write your target word in all capital letters, then remove any duplicates so that the letters appear in your string letters only once.
3. Break out and isolate the shapes of those letters so that only the rudimentary unduplicated shapes are represented. If there are two or sets of letters, do this each set.
4. Use these shapes to construct a sigil for that target word. Try multiple and different approaches to constructing a single graphic figure for the set of shapes.
5. Once the graphic sigil is fashioned, you can embellish it to make it look more esthetically pleasing.

6. Perform these steps against each of the words in your list until each one is represented by a graphic sigil. Now you have the foundation of an alphabet of aspiration and can use it to formulate sigil sentences for any magical objective you might seek to realize.

Spare's magic techniques for the construction of sigils, pictograms, mantras. and an alphabet of aspirations is an ingenious methodology for developing a magical link between the subject and target in a magical working. It is concise, efficient, and very effective. I have been using these methods in my magical workings for decades, since I first read Frater U. D.'s book *Practical Sigil Magic* when it was published in 1990. I have taught this technique to other folks, and they have also found it useful and quite powerful. I consider it one of the more important tools in the toolbox for the magical notary art, hence its prominence in this book.

However, there are other techniques that we should examine, since a toolbox will often have many tools to be used depending on the situation and the need. There is the use of magical alphabets to embellish labels and deity names, and there are the medieval nota that were used in the grimoire *Ars Notoria* that can be brought into use in our modern age. Let us continue this exposition.

CHAPTER SIX

MAGICAL ALPHABETS: A BRIEF OVERVIEW

THE USE OF MAGICAL ALPHABETS has a long and venerable history, but it became a more varied practice during the Renaissance than it was in antiquity. This is likely due to the fact that as time progressed, more people became literate, and there was a need to make titles and labels for the names of spirits and deities more obscure and embellished. Magical languages are implied in the use of occult alphabets, and there are the early attempts at creating ciphers and letter substitutions that would hide the true meaning and importance of certain names and words of power from outsiders. In some cases, the alphabets used were so fabulous looking and had a fake patina of antiquity that they could function as a form of sigil writing, similar to the alphabet of aspirations that we discussed in the previous chapter.

However, as ciphers go, simple letter substitution was not much of a disguise for writing since an analysis of the pattern of letter use would make it easy to resolve by intelligent scrutiny. By the time of Elizabethan England, spies were using much more sophisticated methods of disguising their writing than simply using a simple alphabet letter substitution. It would seem, then, that these alphabets were used to embellish and empower names and phrases, so it could be seen as a kind of esthetic and artistic technique of enhancing and slightly obscuring words and names.

One of the most famous magical alphabets, and one that became a favorite of Witches in 1960s and 1970s, was the Theban alphabet. My first encounter with this script was in the book *Mastering Witchcraft*, where it was variously called the "Witches' alphabet," "Witches' runes," or "runes of Honorius" (a reputed Theban magician), but in later illustrations in the book, the Witch tools were inscribed with these letters.[22]

A	B	C	D	E	F	G	H
I,J	K	L	M	N	O	P	Q
R	S	T	U,V,W	X	Y	Z	.

Francis Barrett, in the book *The Magus*, had this alphabet along with magical scripts based on the Hebrew letters. These were known as Celestial writing, Malachim writing, and another set called Passing of the River.[23] There was also the Enochian alphabet, Ogham, Norse Runes, and many others far more obscure. Basically, it was nothing more than substituting a known letter for one from a magical alphabet to use for deity names, spirit names, and magical words of power. Any kind of artistic or mystical

---

22   Huson, Paul, *Mastering Witchcraft* (G. P. Putnam and Sons, 1970) p. 41.
23   Tyson, Donald, *Three Books of Occult Philosophy* (Llewellyn Publications, 1992) p. 563. Plate showing alphabets from *The Magus*.

alphabet would work, as long as the magician knew what they spelled, and, of course, for those who didn't know, the words would appear mysterious and arcane.

I have known some who have used Tolkien's Elven or Dwarven alphabets in their magical cryptography, and all of it has a certain esthetic appeal. The rationale for using these substituted alphabets is to embellish and obscure the various names or words of power that one is employing in a magic temple, personal grimoires, or magical scripts. Adding another layer to an obscure discipline requires that you practice the replacement script often and extensively so that it becomes second nature to observe, read, and recite. Without this degree of familiarity, adopting this kind of replacement script becomes a clumsy affectation, which greatly diminishes the esthetic effect.

As for myself, I never bothered to take on one of these alphabets. I instead used a whole different interesting way of writing magical runes or glyphs, believing that I discovered the writing style of ancient Atlantis, although that was more inspirational than provable. When I was still a teenager and a newly minted Witch (by my own hand), I came up with a whole system of magic using my boundless imagination and the scant reading materials available at the time, but over time, I abandoned it for the more sophisticated and deep traditional magical lore. Still, I understand that creativity and the powers of the imagination are crucial to any magical development, so I still possess all my writings and notes from that time so long ago.

So, if you feel very attracted to a specialized writing script and feel the passionate urge to master it and to use it in your magical work, then a period of rigorous practice awaits you. Once you have mastered a magical alphabet, then the question becomes, what is the best application for such a technique?

I have used magical alphabets to label the statues, pictures, and sigils of deities and spirits and make them quite presentable and beautifully deployed in my temple. Using this technique, a magician would write the translated name on a piece of parchment or inscribe it on a piece of wood or metal, and then consecrate and charge it so that it is sacralized. Then place it next to the statue, picture, or artifact so that only the magician who wrote it will know the name and the identity of that entity.

You can employ the same process to sacred or secret names in your personal grimoire, using special ink and consecrating it so that it becomes a kind of magical hyperlink to that entity if it is pointed at or touched and the obscured name vibrated or intoned. This can be done to words of power so that they are hidden in magical books, but also sacralized and empowered. This can also be done with tools, where they are engraved with the names and words of power and then consecrated. There are a lot of different things that can be done once a magical alphabet is mastered, but to be effective, it *must* be fully mastered.

While this use of magical alphabets can have a great esthetic appeal, I have found that using such a methodology can accidentally make a grimoire more difficult to read, especially if the alphabet is not exercised for a period of time. I believe that embellishing labels for deities is probably a good use for this technique, but overall, I think that it could be overused and, at some point, force the magician to have to re-acquire the alphabet. For this reason, I have used this approach sparingly and more for decoration and its esthetic appeal than to hide the names of deities and spirits.

However, developing magical names can also be an important device in ritual work, and this where the use acronyms and formula names becomes an important technique to consider.

MAGICAL FORMULAS AND LETTER TO NUMBER TRANSLATIONS

Magical formulas and names often do not have any inherent meaning, since they are typically developed or derived for a specific magical purpose. Sometimes they are corruptions or actual words or phrases, and other times they are magical words of power. *Abracadabra* is one example, and *AGLA* or *INRI* are others. Although sometimes meanings can be derived from these words (or they might be acronyms), their effect when expressed is more important than their meaning—if they have any meaning.

An important consideration is that there has been a precedence of seeing numbers as representing the mathematical elements of sacred geometry. This sacred geometry represents the true and hidden structure to the spiritual dimensions and was the topic explored by Pythagoras in his occult philosophies. Numbers, then, have an inherent meaning, since they represent the factors used by the Deity as Creator to fashion the universe of spirit, mind, and matter. The relationship between numbers and letters, and how they have been developed into a unified metaphysical teaching, symbolizes the core concept that thought becomes material form, and material form becomes thought, which is the very premise of transformative magic. If the mind is the bridge between this material and spiritual reality, then numbers and words are the stones and steel that make up this bridge. Thus, the art of translating letters of words into numbers represents how words consisting of letters are associated with numbers—the key to mathematics and geometry—thereby associating sacred texts with sacred geometry.

It is for this reason that the Qabalists developed techniques to translate letters into numbers, establish systems of using ciphers to obscure words of power or discover hidden words in sacred texts, and craft acronyms that hold empowered phrases or discover the words behind sacred acronyms and thereby explode them into meaningful phrases. These are the language-based techniques known as Gematria, Notariqon, and Temurah, and they should become important practical tools when developing and working with formulas and magical words of power, or determining the occult relationship between words through their numeric value. However, Jewish Qabalists were not the only ones who used technique of number and letter substitution, since the Greeks used a similar approach using letters to denote numbers in their writings. It is possible that they may have borrowed and developed their methodologies from the Greeks.

Therefore, the notary art can be used to investigate formulas, words of power, and specialized names so that they can be subjected to the translation into numbers and then compared or exploded out from initials or acronyms, or formed from a phrase and reduced to an acronym. This art form of translating letters to numbers,

numbers to letters, substituting one set of letters for another, and creating or expanding acronyms is an important part of working with letters and words in magical rituals. While we can borrow the techniques of the Qabalists, some of these techniques are more useful than others; we will focus on those and briefly cover the others. Still, it is up to you how far into this practice you will seek to go, and there are always other, deeper sources of information for you to study.[24]

The art of Gematria, where letters are associated with numbers and added together to determine the relative numeric value of words, is useful and interesting if one is examining key words in sacred writings. It requires the creation of a Sepher Sephiroth, or book of numbers, where words with the same values can be grouped together and compared. I have found this approach somewhat interesting, but occult authors have overused this technique to equate words and therefore offer proof of underlying meaning which is, in my opinion, a bridge too far. Temurah is a practical system of letter substitution for the creation of ciphers or to decrypt words and sentences from sacred texts. Other than the AIQ BKR table, this is a branch of working with letters and words that we can cite but don't need to pursue. That leaves us with Notariqon, which is the art of building and exploding acronyms, and it is here where we will examine this simple technique that has quite a number of uses in ritual construction.

We have already shown that letter substitution is an important part of working with magical squares, and the AIQ BKR table and the association of numbers with Hebrew letters have been discussed in the chapter concerning magical squares. However, Notariqon, the specific artistic technique to craft acronym formulas and explode them into phrases is something we should cover here, since working with acronyms is the basis of developing and using formula words.

---

[24] Crowley, Aleister, *777 and Other Qabalistic Writings of Aleister Crowley* (Samuel Weiser, 1973) edited by Israel Regardie, pp. 1–26. Crowley has an entire section covering the different systems of the Qabalah for Gematria, Notariqon, and Temurah.

The use of formula words and acronyms was first shown in the Golden Dawn ritual of the Rose Cross, in the Analysis of the Keyword, and I would recommend the reader to examine it in full.[25] While this rite comes at the end of the ritual and is an exposition of the famous acronyms INRI (Jesus of Nazareth, King of the Jews) and LVX (Light), where these formulas are emphasized with body postures emulating the letters, they could also have been used to define the points in the circle where the Rose Cross is drawn and expressed with the sacred godhead names. This is the methodology that I have adopted from an analysis of this ritual. The Rose Cross ritual also produces a kind of vortex energy field, which is a plus.

To expand this kind of formula use, I set a letter, word, and concept at each point within the magic circle, and at the end, perform a kind of keyword analysis where the letters form a formula word through the recapitalization of the words that were set to the points in the circle. This creates a recursive structure where the elements of the ritual are pulled together at the end to form an acronym formula that lends a unified meaning and ideation to the ritual actions.

I have found that using this approach causes a set of points or nodes in a ritual structure to be powerfully unified, becoming a unitary structure in the ritual. The combination of letters may form an acronym word, or they might just represent a formula that has no definition. The function of acronyms or formulas is to create unitary structures, and a set of unitary structures are layered one upon the other to formulate a ritual. I have adopted a rigorous approach to using acronyms to pull together the parts of ritual into structural unity. We should briefly examine this approach since it makes rituals more concise and gives them a continuity that they might otherwise lack.

The first example starts out with a formula word that represents the godhead of the element Water and the Qabalistic world of Briah. I am seeking to set the element attributes of water to the four Watchtowers and qualify them with a four-fold formula representing the Qabalistic world of Briah. I chose the formula of

---

25 Regardie, Israel, *The Golden Dawn 7th Edition* (Llewellyn Publications, 2016) edited by John Michael Greer, p. 390.

ShDAY to represent the godhead name of Shaddai El Chai, the Lord of Life, and used these four letters and their association to build the overall formula word.

Beginning in the East, I draw the device, vibrate the letter Shin, make other declarations, and specify that Shin represents the Great Spirit. I then proceed to the South, where I perform various ritual actions, vibrate the letter Daleth, make other declarations, and specify that Daleth is the great Throne or Khursia, which is the primary symbolic representation of the Qabalistic world of Briah. I proceed to the West, perform the various ritual actions, vibrate the letter Aleph, and specify that it represents the creative act of formulation (magic). I proceed to the North, perform various rituals actions, vibrate the letter Yod, and specify that it represents the creative plane or world. Then, when I proceed to the center of the circle, I perform the keyword analysis, identifying and pulling the components of the four letter formula together to form the letters of the godhead of Briah, which is *Shadai*, and I declare an exegesis of that word representing the union of the four concepts of Great Spirt, throne, creative will, and the world of creation to characterize the domain of Briah.

Another example uses the Greek letters and words to generate a formula that captures the essence of the theme of the ritual, which is crossing the wasteland of the desert of culture and diminished ideals to arrive at the oasis of truth hidden within it. The keyword represents what is sacrificed to achieve this quest, and the formula letters represent the fourfold stages of that process. This is very complex ritual, but these five points of the magic circle, the four Watchtowers, and the center of the circle are qualified to pull the meaning parts or stages of the internal truth together into a concise unified concept.

In the ritual, the operator sets a pylon device to the four Watchtowers consisting of an invoking pentagram of receptive (feminine) spirit to the base and a hexagram device of union at the apex. This is done to each of the Watchtowers; however, each Watchtower is qualified by the formula letter, word, and declaration that makes each unique. I have used parts of the poem "The Wasteland" by T. S. Eliot to represent the passage of the initiate. The structure of formula letters and words, set to the four Watchtowers, have the following meaning.

1. **East:** Alpha—*Autokrator*—Absolute (the One)
2. **South:** Iota—*Ilasmos*—Atonement
3. **West:** Mu—*Mantikos*—Prophecy (system of magic)
4. **North:** Omicron—*hOrkion*—Oath

Combining the Greek letters A, I, M, and O reveals the formula of the ritual, which is the prefix *Aimo-*, meaning "blood." These letters and words represent a process of internal reduction, purification, and spiritual alignment to the concept of the One that is None, the exemplification of emptiness that represents the core of the desert and its impact on the mind of the initiate who adopts this quest to seek the ultimate truth. While that might seem very deep and complex—and it is—this example shows how powerful the use of formulas as acronyms can be and how much information can be condensed into a simple expression. *Aimo* in this example becomes a word of power because of the layers of meaning and context that have become associated with it.

Using acronym formulas embedded in a ritual represents the methodology that I employ to give a unifying theme and concept to the parts of rituals. I can also write multiple layers in my rituals, each with a key word analysis, and the overall ritual structure that joins those layers together using a combined key word analysis. I can unify a series of rituals or the structure of a ritual so that the overall concept and meaning can be encapsulated by a single formula word. That allows the magician to express an entire working in a single word and concept, which means that they could employ just those condensed formula words to express an entire array of ritual workings. That is something to contemplate when writing rituals, since building in a kind of macro-ritual into a ritual structure can allow one to reacquire the energy and intelligences generated in a working through a simple set of actions and adopting a deep meditative state.

An acronym formula does not have to be a word that has meaning in some language to be a potent magical word of power, and, in fact, it is the practice of ritual workings that will ultimately give a formula its meaning and context. This is one of the methods for generating a body of words and acronyms that have a very specific meaning and effect when used in a powerful and altered state of consciousness.

Thus, this formula-building is a very important technique in the notary art, where the magician uses words and letters to build ritual formulas, which embody a special contextual meaning and can encapsulate magical powers and materialized effects. I have taken a simple example used by the Golden Dawn, and through the notary art, made it into a powerful mechanism in the art of ritual magic.

CHAPTER SEVEN

MAGICAL NOTARIES: A BRIEF OVERVIEW

ONE OF THE MOST INTERESTING and curious magical grimoires from the late medieval period was the book *Ars Notoria: the Notary Art of Solomon the King*. This book was likely developed in the late thirteenth century, so it predates many of the later and more famous grimoires. It was a kind of psalter or prayer book that had prayers invoking angelic names and used various *verba ignota* or barbarous words of evocation to assist clerics in mastering the arts and sciences. It was through the operation of magical liturgical rites that such knowledge would become available to the mind of the adherent, yet it would only add to the liturgical responsibilities that a cleric and member of the church hierarchy would already be expected to perform. The spectrum of knowledge and understanding gained through the recitation of these prayers would cover the entire coursework of the trivium and quadrivium, including what would be considered post-graduate studies, such medicine, philosophy, law, and theology.[26]

Aside from the magical prayers contained in the book, there were great symbolic figures and geometric shapes where these prayers and words of power and evocation were integrated into designs, creating what were called *magical nota* (plural *notae*). It was these illuminated

---

26   Skinner, Stephen, *Ars Notoria: The Method Version B: Mediaeval Angel Magic* (Llewellyn Publications, 2021) p. 14–15.

designs, with figures of angels, tables, sigils, and various prayers and words of invocation integrated into an array of geometric structures, that made this grimoire unique. The prayers and words of invocation are still, to this day, extremely effective and resonant. They have a powerful magical effect, which I know because I have used them in my magical ritual workings. Yet, taken out of the context of the actual notae or geometric structures will likely lessen their potency, which is to say that they would be ever-more powerful if they were kept in the context of the nota where they appear.

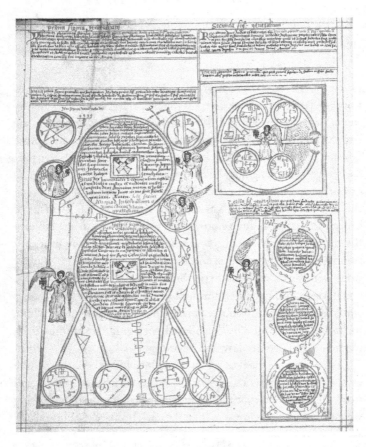

*Example of the 6th Nota of Astronomy
as taken from the Ars Noteria*

Of course, no one today has one of these illuminated manuscripts in their possession, because they are old, rare, and, by now, extremely fragile; therefore, they cannot be used in today's world as a kind of iconic talismanic magic to gain knowledge and insights. While there are printed versions of these various nota, you would need to produce a volume where they are large enough and printed in color to use as a magical workbook. Such an edition is not available at time of writing.

When these psalters became popular to the literati of the time, medieval biblical scholars believed that the highest level of knowledge one could attain was not in the topical areas of mathematics, logic, rhetoric, or medicine. Theology, which was considered even higher than the philosophy of the Pagans, reigned supreme amongst the pedagogy of the time. One could conceivably approach the acquisition of a knowledge of theology through the use of magic without being too far off course. In our post-modern world, theology is no longer quite as important compared to the hard sciences, law, medicine, and even the soft sciences of anthropology, sociology, linguistics, psychology, and numerous others.

While it could be conceivable that a student in the Middle Ages might use a magical methodology to open their mind and grasp the various concepts of the time's collective knowledge, it is likely too great a task to even consider in our modern age. Instead of a religious magic used to open up the door of the mind, we have tutors and online teaching systems that can help the more dim-witted of our student population to achieve academic credentials. It would seem that the magical workings and psalters of notae have no place in our modern world, which is likely why this grimoire has not been as popular as other and later works, such as the *True Grimoire*, to the current crowd of grimoire aficionados.

Still, obtaining insights and realizations about spiritual and occult topics through magical operations is a relevant approach, no better or worse than any other method. I have gained an enormous volume of occult knowledge and spiritual insights using the art of magic, although, in most instances, it aids my ability to convince others when these insights are grounded or supported by other sources of knowledge. While I would not seek to gain the body of knowledge accumulated in our current age through the application of magic by itself, I could consider that inspiration and thinking outside the box would be facilitated by very specific magical operations. Sometimes, no matter how hard we strive to understand a topic, it remains opaque to us until something in our mind allows us to make connections and realizations that remove the blockage to full understanding. These are the likely places where magic can be used to expand a person's overall understanding and help them to acquire new instruction.

I believe that the effective use of notae and words of power is to help the mind to become flexible, open, and capable of realizing new ideas and teachings. It is a kind of linguistic game to make the mind flexible, malleable, and inspired to learn new topics, especially ones that would seem foreign or unrelated to the kind of knowledge that one already possesses.

When approaching a difficult subject, it is often necessary to overcome personal bias and beliefs that are difficult or even impossible to understand. I have had this kind of bias against learning advanced forms of mathematics, even though I have developed a very logical and organized mind to program computers. A friend, who is a master of mathematics, has told me that my bias was instilled by poor teachers and poorly written books, and that armed with better books and an inspiring teacher, that bias would disappear. I would think that magic could also undo prejudices and biases against certain topics that individuals would believe are beyond their capabilities. This is where I think that the medieval notary art could find a niche in the modern practice of magic.

The question that I should probably answer is, how do we use the notae from the *Ars Noteria* if the whole pedagogical process is wholly and completely different in our day and age? If each magical nota is set to a specific discipline in the teaching syllabus of the Middle Ages, then how would we apply them to our magical workings today? I think that some of them might be applicable, but only remotely as an aid to mastering a new intellectual discipline. Also, the magical prayers are still usable when applied to magical workings, but their specific purpose and use has to be modified and altered to fit a new magical context.

Thus, I believe that the usefulness of this magical psalter is found in using parts of it to augment ritual workings with invocative, barbarous words of power. One can use a bit of selectivity to reuse this lore in a completely different manner, similar to the appropriation of the evocations from the *PGM,* where much of the context of those spells and some of their components are not useful nor acceptable. I have used this approach and found that the words of power work exceptionally well, and they can be adapted to ritual contexts that are quite different from their original spells.

Perhaps the best approach is to define exactly what the nota are and how they work, and using that knowledge, create our own versions of these magical spells to use in our modern ritual workings. In taking this approach, we might return to our regimen the techniques of a medieval magic that has long passed out of use.

A magical nota is a combination of magical words of power and prayers or exhortations placed into a geometric design and printed or drawn on parchment, where it is consecrated and charged as one would do to a sigil. You can—and should—make the image like a page from an illuminated manuscript, with other sigils and images of spirits, angels, or demons incorporated into the design. Once it is beautifully crafted and consecrated, it can be used as a kind of magical icon graphically representing a magical operation.

Regarding the words of power, prayer, and exhortation, you can use any traditional words of power from grimoires (or even from the *Ars Noteria* itself), or you can write it in a magical language (such as Enochian), disguise certain words with a magical alphabet, translate the whole set of words into that alphabet, or you can just write in your own vernacular. As I have stated, writing English words in a powerful exhortation is often more than enough to use in fashioning a magical nota. I have found that just transferring a powerful English exhortation into a geometric design and using plain pen and ink to write it on a piece of parchment and then consecrating it is all that is needed. Sometimes, the simplest approach can be just as powerful as incorporating magical alphabets, illumination techniques, and sigils and the like into a much more elaborate nota. Because it is a matter of esthetics, it becomes your choice how you proceed, as long as you follow the basic ideas of what makes a magical nota into a powerful artifact.

A magical nota incorporates many of the skills associated with the notary art, which would be formulating words of power, developing geometric structures, and loading them with words of power, prayers, and magical exhortations. It could also incorporate magical alphabets, sigils of aspirations, and sigils of the names of spirits. All these art forms work together to create a magical icon that would be used in a ritual to activate a specific magical process or unleash powers and intelligences, or a combination of these, encapsulated into an esthetic graphic presentation. Thus, all of the techniques that we have been discussing in this book could be employed to create a powerful magical nota.

I believe that the magical nota is a very powerful tool and artifact that can be employed in magical workings or used by itself to project magical processes and produce tangible material results. I have worked with these kinds of magical artifacts for decades and I have found them to be the most powerful tools that I have ever used. A well-designed and deployed nota can have a greater magical effect than any single sigil construct because it contains and encapsulates many different elements into a single graphical design.

It is my hope that this brief exposition defines and shows examples of magical nota that have been produced using English in a modern context and will inspire other magicians to take this approach and develop their own artifacts. I believe that this method of magic, which employs many of the notary arts into a single practice, is likely the most potent magical representation that anyone could develop. While the *Ars Noteria* might not be very useful in its antique manuscript form, it can and does represent a magical technique that is still relevant today. It is one that I recommend that you investigate and adapt to your magical repertoire.

Here are some examples of magical nota that I have produced. One is from a series of unpublished rituals where I establish the context of the nota at the end of a complex and very intense ritual working. The other was an icon that I crafted while completely in trance, and it represents another kind of magical nota that can be created, employing a form of direct visualization and automatic writing.

This is the magical nota that I use to encapsulate a ritual working:

Philathea
   Philathea
      Philathea

   The Refinement
      Of Atmosphere
      Regards its reflection
      Reflecting

   O Charis Kai Aletheia
   Unity throughout the
   L I G H T!

   Sanos Charissimus
   Ramos Charissimus
   Danos Charissimus
*   *Aliyah Hagios Phaos*   *

The Pure Gentle
   Of silent sense
   Is like brilliance
   The splendor of brilliance!

ALL LIGHT ULTRA CONSCIOUSNESS

ELAH
LAO   *AROT*
IAH   *TARO*
ZAO   *ROTA*
EHI   *OTAR*
   BETHEL   AUMYAHUMMANNAA +
      ELOHIM   AUMYAHUMMANNAA +
         THELIEL   AUMYAHUMMANNAA +

Here is an example of an icon variation of a magical nota, used as gateway seal for the Nephilim workings:

If you are interested in knowing more about the grimoire *Ars Noteria*, then I would recommend the book *Ars Notoria: The Method Version B: Mediaeval Angel Magic* written by Dr. Stephen Skinner. The author not only explores the historical context of this grimoire, but there are also colored plates showing what the various notae look like in the rare grimoires that exist in collections.

PART III

RITES OF SIGIL, SEAL, NOTAE, AND SIGNATURE CONSECRATION

CHAPTER EIGHT

CONSECRATING AND CHARGING SIGILS, SEALS, AND NOTAE

WE HAVE COVERED ALL THE VARIOUS MECHANISMS for producing sigils, seals, and notae, and it is assumed that you will take these designs and apply them to some kind of medium. You can use pen and ink, colored markers, paints, or enamels, and apply the designs to parchment paper, tag board, plywood, or metal badges or discs.

What you *should* use is a semi-permanent or permanent artistic medium of some kind to apply the design so that it will withstand some handling and use. The more indestructible or permanent the application and the surface upon which it is applied, the longer life cycle such an artifact will have. Parchment sigils are often disposable, and they can be burned to release the magical powers and intelligences that they represent. What you use to craft an artifact will determine its use and also the method of consecrating and charging it.

It is likely that you will engage in developing your artistic imagination and ability to craft sigils and seals by using a variety of mediums and application surfaces. That is an area you will have to explore and develop outside of this work. I won't talk about how you should craft your magical tools, but I will talk about how to empower and use them in your magical rites. Once you have crafted a sigil, seal, or nota, then you will need to consecrate and charge it, and this chapter will focus on the various techniques, rituals, and workings that you will use to transform and activate a magical artifact, making it ready for use.

I will assume that you know the basics of consecrating a tool or artifact, but I will present in this chapter some rituals that will help to perform that task, and you can modify them or use rituals that you have developed instead. What I am presenting is very basic, so if a more elaborate ritual approach is part of your magical esthetics, then you can take these rituals and elaborate them however you wish.

Consecration is the act of taking an object and, through the artifice of ritual, making it holy. It is a process of sacralization that transforms or transubstantiates a substance so that it is imbued with the essence of Spirit. While consecration can be conferred by using an object in a magical context, a more formal approach is taken to confer a special and direct sacralization for objects that are to become magical tools. The dagger and wand are formally consecrated, as are necklaces and other jewelry, but temple furniture, candle holders, chalices, and thuribles are consecrated by use.

Similar to the science behind making a magnet from a bar of iron, applying substances that have been consecrated to an unconsecrated object will make it *sacralized*. Applying sacramental substances to the object thereby makes it holy through contagion. We should briefly discuss how this works and how it might be applied to different types of magical tools, especially sigils, seals, and notae.

USE OF SACRAMENTS FOR CONSECRATION

Magical tools and artifacts are consecrated using sacraments. While it is typical that Witches and Pagans, and even ceremonial magicians, use food and drink to make offerings to their Deities and request the return of such substances for the purpose of communion with those Godheads, there is often little understanding that these substances have been altered through intervention into substances that have inherent magical powers. Instead of drinking and eating these sacraments, a magician can use them to sacralize other objects.

There are four sacraments that are generated in the basic magical and liturgical operations. The first is lustral water, which is a mixture of salt and water that is used similarly to holy water to sacralize the temple and prepare it for laying and inscribing the magic circle. The second and third sacraments are the wine and bread used in the communion rite after the drawing down or godhead assumption rite. The fourth is the oil or balm that is used in initiations. Additionally, there is the burnt offering as incense smoke, and the light or flame of an altar candle.

However, central to these sacraments is the operator, who performs the rites of blessing and charging. In this act of blessing and charging, they will make a sign (such as a cross, ankh, or hexagram) over the object, focus their bodily energy on it with their hand, and then lean down and blow their breath upon it. If the operator is working under the influences of a light godhead assumption, then this process of sacralizing is using the agency of Deity to make it a magical transformative process. The charged sacraments are imbued with the essence of that Deity, and thus they belong to it. The operator mentally offers these sacraments to the Deity, and they are graciously returned to be used. The operator, as a surrogate for the Deity, performs this operation of sacralization so that the products of that activity can be used to bless people and other objects.

Therefore, consecrating a tool or artifact is little more than applying sacraments to that object, depending on the material from which it is constructed. The operator will apply sacraments to an object but will also, standing as a surrogate for the Deity, apply the holy sign, projected charge, and the breath blown upon it as the final mechanism for fully imbuing it with the essence of the spirit of that godhead. All tools and artifacts are consecrated in the name of a specific godhead and through that entity's agency, so they belong to that spiritual being and are used as a form of gracious return to the hands and mind of the magician.

Certain artifacts require the application of specific sacraments to make them consecrated. Some of this is common sense, while others may not be as well known. Here are the various combinations of sacraments used to consecrate the classes of sacralized objects. Most artifacts will be placed in category two or four, but I thought a full list would be appropriate to list here.

1. **Medicines, oils, ointments, or potions:** touched delicately with a host or bread fragment, then the operator makes a sign over it and blows breath upon it.
2. **Tools, sigils, seals, notae, amulets, pre-charged talismans, or any metal or wood objects:** touched with a host or bread fragment, lustral water and/or wine, or consecrated oil (wiped off afterward) and exposed to incense smoke, then the operator makes a sign over it and blows breath upon it.
3. **Vestments, stole/scarf, hat, cape, phylacteries, bandages, or any object made of cloth:** touched with a host fragment, a light sprinkling of lustral water (wiped off afterward), and exposed to incense smoke, then the operator makes a sign over it and blows breath upon it.
4. **Sigils for evocation, or any parchment or paper object:** touched with a host fragment, exposed to incense smoke, and touched briefly with a small metal wand that has been exposed to lustral water or wine, then the operator makes a sign over it and blows breath upon it.

Knowing these different methods for consecrating an object is important so that the action doesn't damage, stain, or ruin it. These are common sense methods, and they might vary depending on the object's material. However, the overall structure of the special rite of sacramental consecration will not change regardless of the material of the target object. The one exception is for sigils used for spirit names. These I will mark with a droplet of sacramental wine and allow it to carefully dry without damaging the sigil design.

METHODS OF CHARGING AND CONSECRATION

Rituals that consecrate and empower artifacts are simple rites that require the use of sacraments and the light godhead assumption associated with magical workings. The place where sacraments are generated and kept are in a temple, and any kind of consecration needs to be performed in sacred space, so a circle consecration rite should be performed in a temple before the rite of consecration is to be performed.

I will assume that the operator has liturgical rites to consecrate the sacraments that will be used to consecrate and charge a sigil, seal, or nota. These can be as simple as a drawing down rite and communion, where the wine and bread fragments are saved for use in a consecration rite. Another approach is to use a mass rite and benediction rite to generate the sacraments and sacralize the temple prior to performing the consecration rite. The mechanism for producing the sacraments is completely your decision and is based on the liturgical rituals that you use as your religious practice. However, I will borrow a ritual that I have published in the book *Sacramental Theurgy for Witches* that is the best example of how to perform this kind of operation.[27] You can also find in that book Pagan-based mass and benediction rites.

RITE OF SACRAMENTAL CONSECRATION[28]

This rite is performed once the magical mass and benediction rites have been completed, or whatever is used to create sacraments. Whatever is to be consecrated is placed on or near the altar, where the sacraments that will be used are arrayed before the veiled chalice in dishes or vials. The celebrant is the same who performed the mass and benediction, and therefore is inspired by the powers

---

27   Frater Barrabbas, *Sacramental Theurgy for Witches* (Crossed Crow Books, 2024) chapter 9, p. 115–132; chapter 10, pp. 133–142.
28   Frater Barrabbas, *Sacramental Theurgy for Witches* (Crossed Crow Books, 2024) pp. 149–152. I have taken this rite and produced it here for consecrating various notary artifacts.

and grace of the Deity. That Deity is identified only with a place marker as "X," since it will be replaced by the Deity name under whose authority you are blessing the artifact.

If the object is an oil, ointment, elixir, potion, or medicine, the Celebrant removes the cover from its container, revealing the contents within. The wand that is used to apply a droplet of sacrament is short and small, three inches in length. A small spoon or stick could also be used.

The Celebrant stands before the object to be consecrated in front of the altar, raises their arms to the heavens, and says the following exhortation:

> *O God/dess, whose name is [X], I am here before your shrine to bless this artifact [Y] in your name. May your holy flesh, blood, tears, breath, and kiss be used to elevate this artifact, so that it will be imbued with your essence; a spark of your spirit will dwell in this holy container so long as it remains in sacred trust.*

They take a fragment of bread or host from the dish upon the altar between the thumb and index finger and make the appropriate sign over the object, then touch it three times. (This is for all objects to be consecrated.)

> *I first bless you with the flesh of the God/dess [X], so that you are made sacred and holy.*

They take up the lit and burning thurible from the altar and make the appropriate sign with it over the object, and then circle the thurible around and over it three times. (This is for all objects to be consecrated.)

> *I twice bless you with the fragrant burnt offerings of the God/dess [X], so that you are made sacred and holy.*

They bow before the object on the altar and make the sign over it, then touch it, projecting the power of the Deity onto it, and then blow their breath into and over the object.

I thrice bless you with the holy sign, touch, and breath of the God/dess [X], so that you are made sacred and holy. Let the essence of God/dess [X] reside within you and be a light in the darkness for all time.

If lustral water is to be used, the Celebrant takes the small wand, dips it into the container of lustral water, and sprinkles a tiny amount on the surface of the object. (If the object requires less water, then touching the wand to the object shall suffice.) They say:

I bless you with the holy tears of the God/dess [X], so that you are made sacred and holy.

If consecrated oil is to be used, the Celebrant takes their finger and dips it into the sacred oil and applies it to the surface of the object. (It is wiped clean with a cloth after the blessing is completed.) They say:

I bless you with the balm of oil from the body of the God/dess [X], so that you are made sacred and holy.

If consecrated wine is to be used, the Celebrant takes the small wand and dips it into the vial of wine and deposits a small drip upon the object. (Depending on whether it is a tool or sigil, it will be wiped clean with a cloth or left to stain the parchment.) They say:

I bless you with the blood from the body of the God/dess [X], so that you are made sacred and holy.

Once the sacrament has been used to charge and bless the artifact, the Celebrant holds out their hands over their head and then brings them down to touch the object, perceiving the power of the Deity passing from the sacralized environment into the object. They say:

You are blessed and charged three-fold with the essence of the God/dess [X], whose spark now resides fully within you. I shall ensure that this spark is loved and fed with the magical work that I take upon myself, and gift it to the world at large so that the light of the Spirit shall be ever greater by one in the World. So mote it be!

If the artifact is an amulet, then the Celebrant will hold it for a while in their hand and identify the person to whom this godhead jewel is being gifted, as well as its function and purpose.

The Celebrant will then put away the dishes and vials of sacrament, and they will fumigate the altar and the temple one more time. The artifact will be carefully wrapped up and put away so that it might incubate for forty-eight hours before being used or given to its recipient. If the artifact is any kind of vestment, it will be hung up in a dark closet for the incubation period.

TRIPLE CONSECRATION FOR SPIRIT OR GODHEAD PLACEHOLDERS

Only in the case of consecrating and charging a name label or signature for a Deity will the consecration rite be performed three times over a consecutive period of days. The operator may also bless a nota in this fashion as well.

For the best results, I would recommend that the consecration be performed before the Moon is full while it is waxing, and that the final rite should be done on or just before the full moon. Then this artifact should be covered up and allow it to incubate in darkness for a period of seventy-two hours, which would be the same number of hours for a talisman to incubate.

A truly thrice-consecrated artifact has the special quality of being supercharged with the essence of the Deity; therefore, it can function as a place marker or surrogate representative of the Deity. If a nota is thrice-consecrated, then it is fully activated and becomes a doorway between the spirit world of the Deity and the material world of the magician. Such a doorway can be used to make a true passage between worlds, allowing the powers of the Deity and the symbolic construct of the nota to project its powers and intelligences into the material world of the magician.

Experimenting with thrice-consecrated artifacts will teach you how to make activated portals between the worlds of spirit and matter, representing a kind of theurgic magic that is highly impactful and able to readily manifest the spiritual powers and authorities of the Deity into the world. There is no better form of magic than this, and it is one of the higher aspects of working the notary art of magic.

Once a sigil, seal, or nota artifact is consecrated and charged, then it can be used in a number of different types of magical operations. In some cases, the artifact can be used by itself to bend the probabilities of material reality and open a door between worlds. When used in a working, it becomes the focus or fulcrum for effectively achieving the purpose of the rite.

A sigil and a seal make the rites of invocation and evocation much more effective and successful; a sigil significantly increases the ability to bind energy fields to a given objective or purpose, a nota artifact opens the doors of perception in a ritual using the psychological model of magic, and as a talismanic artifact, it suspends time to mark the moment as auspicious when working planetary magic. The notary art makes ritual workings using other magical models more effective and successful and can function as magical artifacts that can be wielded as powers by themselves.

We should proceed to the next chapter, where I will show the many ways to employ the notary art in different kinds of ritual workings, and where it already has a place in some of them. We should also note that the information model of magic has a place for this kind of magical artifact, which can be used to impress the magician's will on material reality and open doors between worlds to aid in the process of self-realization and personal gnosis.

PART IV

MAGICAL USES OF SIGILS, SEALS, NOTAE, AND SIGNATURES

CHAPTER NINE

FOUNDATIONAL RITES USED IN THE NOTARY ART

In writing this book, I had to assume that you, the reader, already knew how to perform various magical operations using the energy model, the spirit model, and the psychological and temporal models of magic. I have written books that take a deep dive into all of these magical methodologies, but for the sake of ensuring that you understand the mechanics of how to apply the notary art to all of these other models, we should at least briefly cover them here. While the information model of magic can be deployed without having to make use of any other model of magic, even then, there is a baseline of practices and mind-states that should be fully realized in order for that technique of magic to be fully functional.

Developing and producing notary artifacts is a deliberate magical act, and the environment where they are generated, the mind-state of the magician, and even the timing of the work should be fully realized elements. These are subtle qualities that will influence and impact the creation and use of any notary artifact. The very first thing that a magician might want to consider is that the location where the sigil or seal is made should be private—even sequestered.

While it might take time to render a finished artifact carefully and artistically (and in fact some artifacts may take several days or more to complete), keeping a separate room or one that can be used in complete privacy when required is very important. The work should also be kept hidden, along with the artistic tools of the art. What I do is store my unfinished work in a plastic case in my closet along with my artist's storage box to hold my artistic tools. I also spend some time meditating before working on an artifact so that my mind is wholly focused on the work. I would never work on a sigil or seal if I was emotionally unsettled or unable to peacefully focus on it. Whatever is going on in your mind or body will be absorbed into the artifact, so it is important to ensure that only relevant thoughts and impressions should be entertained while doing this work.

MEDITATION IS THE KEY TO THE NOTARY ART

The power of a sigil, seal, signature, placeholder, or notae lies in the realization of its symbolic formulation and how it impacts the mind. These are methods of symbolic communication, but the place where this language has a practical use is in the domain of consciousness that I call the *super-symbolic plane,* or the *conscious collective mind.* Magical powers and energies, spirits, gods and goddesses, angels, demons, heroes and heroines, ancestors, ghosts, monsters, and fantastic beasts all reside in a special place within the collective consciousness of a culture (or humanity in general).

Our world of imagination has as much tangible reality to us as the real world. Sometimes dreams can cross over to become reality, and reality assumes the guise of dreams or nightmares. All of these interlocking psychic elements are pieced together with various forms of language and meaning. Symbols and signs populate this world, and within it are the gateways to what the semiologists might call an *iconic sign,* or the post-language layers of non-verbal forms of higher consciousness.

To gain access to this world, one would use meditation and trance states to travel into this wondrous place. Lucid dreaming is also an important tool, as is scrying and spirit or astral travel. However, we will focus on meditation and trance, since they are the starting point for any notary work. Since meditation is such a basic practice, and one that is integral to any occult work, I will only briefly cover it here. The same is also true for trance techniques. I expect that the student who lacks this training will seek it out from appropriate sources and practice them religiously.

Basic meditation techniques rely on the areas of breath, vision, and hearing. Breath control is the very first technique that one learns to master in the art of meditation. Vision is the second, and it is the key to gaining a trance state. Hearing, the third technique, uses a repetitive chant as a mantra to affect the mind and bring about a deep meditative state.

Breath Control: This technique starts by simply observing your breathing cycle with the mouth closed, noting the inhalation and exhalation of breath through the nose. Then, the next step is to regulate the breathing cycle using an internalized repetitive count. Using an internal count, you will breathe in for the count of four, hold the breath for a count of four, exhale for the count of four, and then hold the lungs empty for the count of four. This is called *the four-fold breathing technique.* You can use any number to count breaths. Additionally, breathing through the mouth with the lips forming an O with a bit of force will produce what I call *cool breathing,* and you can inhale and exhale through the mouth in this manner. This is what I call *projective breath,* and it is used to project magical power onto an object or intensify a ritual action. Another form is to breathe in and out rapidly with the mouth fully open, producing a breathing cycle that is like panting. This is called the *bellows breath,* and it should only be performed for short periods since it can induce dizziness and vertigo when prolonged.

Vision Control: Focusing the eyes on any design or feature and staring at it for long periods of time can induce mild visual illusions, especially when looking at a picture or diagram that uses graphical designs or geometric structures that produce illusions when started at, or illustrations that use contrasting colors, or day-glow painted illustrations that appear three dimensional when looked at under a blacklight. Staring for a prolonged period of time at a blank wall can also induce a trance, especially if one assumes a relaxed mind with the objective of triggering a mild hypnotic state. Guided visualizations and seeking to "see" energy patterns and other obscure occult phenomenon can also be effective while in this state of semitrance. Closing the eyes and adopting a passive form of breath control (observing but not controlling the breath) will deepen a trance state so that one can sense and experience the most subtle internal conscious phenomena. Trance states are self-willed, so they can also be broken by the will to awaken.

Auditory Control: Chanting words or sonorous syllables (such as *aum*) in a continuous and cyclic manner will also promote a meditative state, or, if continued, a deeper trance state. It is an effective technique for mental discipline. Sound has a powerful effect on the mind, and repetitious chanting or the intoning of sacred words, or words of power, will quickly produce the proper mind-state for performing any kind of magical working. For this reason, music can be used to harness the background of one's consciousness and produce a calming and inward-sensing state of mind that is conducive to magical work.

Achieving the correct mind-state is an important precursor to being able to perceive and engage with the energies associated with various notary artifacts. Since sigils, seals, and signs are symbolic qualifiers beyond normal consciousness, only a deep, meditative induced trance state will be sufficient to unlock their powers. A magician uses breath control, breath projection, visualization, and mantra chanting to be able to unlock the powers and direct the qualities of a consecrated sigil, seal, or signature. I would recommend that the student obtain a certain level of mastery of these techniques before attempting to work sigil magic alone without any other accompanied practice.

DIVINATION AND SACRED SPACE

Divination and consecrating one's space are two important practices that you need to know to support the construction and development of an artifact. I believe that it is important that I know the intent of my notary artistic work and that I fully understand everything that is potentially connected to that work. Divination puts eyes on the intention and how that intention would be materially realized. The notary art requires that mundane steps accompany any magical work, unless it is for the realization of occult or spirit-based knowledge, and that the target of the magic is your own mind. My expectation is that you already have the capability to perform divination using more than one system. The use of Tarot cards, rune stones, geomancy sticks, dice, or knucklebones—not to mention knowing some basic astrology—will be part of your regimen for working magic.

Circle consecration can be used to sacralize the process of building a notary artifact, especially if it is a nota or some other kind of sanctified artifact, like the seal of a spirit or a magical relic. For very special operations, it becomes important that the process of developing the artifact is done in a consecrated magical temple or temporary working space. Making an artifact in a consecrated magic circle will greatly impact its potential power and focus its intention in a stronger way than making it anywhere else would have. Adding this component to the process of developing a notary artifact makes sense if the object were to be bonded with a spirit, used as a place marker for a Deity, or fully realized as a specific nota. Unless the end product warrants such an empowered environment, adding additional attributes to an artifact in this manner would only make it more complicated to produce. There is a place for spontaneity and creative flexibility in the creation of sigils and seals, which should be an important consideration as well.

The basic ritual pattern for consecrating a magic circle consists of four basic and consecutive operations. I perform this rite to generate sacred space, but also, in my mind, it replaces the need for the lesser banishing and invoking pentagram rites, producing a sacralized and energized environment. The four steps are generating the lustral water, consecrating the sacred space with the four elements, drawing the magic circle, and setting the four Watchtower invoking pentagrams. Here are the basic steps to performing this ritual:

1. Using a plate with a small amount of salt placed on it and a chalice of spring water, take the magic dagger and touch it to the salt, saying a blessing to make the salt a sacrament. Next, take the dagger and immerse it into the water, feeling energy enter the water, to charge and bless it in the same manner as the salt (thus making it a sacrament). Once that is accomplished, then take the plate of salt and scoop it into the water and, returning the dagger into the combined potion, say a blessing to transform it into lustral water.
2. Take the lustral water and sprinkle small amounts on the floor of the temple, saying a simple prayer and circulating around the circle deosil, starting and ending in the East. Take up a thurible or incense boat with lit, smoking incense and incense the space, starting and ending in the East, while saying a simple prayer. Finally, take a lit candle and show its light to the four cardinal directions, starting and ending in the East.
3. Take the dagger and draw a magic circle, starting and ending in the East. Recite a simple prayer and observe the energy that is illuminating a magic ring around the periphery of the temple.
4. Take the dagger and go to the East, draw an invoking pentagram of Air, and summon the spirit of the Eastern Watchtower. Proceed deosil to the South, drawing an invoking pentagram of Fire, and summon the spirit of the Southern Watchtower. Proceed to the West, drawing an invoking pentagram of Water, and summon the spirit of the Western Watchtower. Proceed to the North, drawing an invoking pentagram of Earth, and summon

the spirit of the Northern Watchtower. The circle and temple are now consecrated.
5. To close the temple, perform banishing pentagrams for the elements of Air to East, Fire to South, Water to West, and Earth to North. Say a prayer of thanksgiving. Only use the banishing rite if there is no vortex set in the magic circle.

Now that we have discussed the need for divination and shown how to build sacred space, we should examine the different methodologies of working magic so that you can fully explore how to choose the right kind of notary artifact to go with a specific kind of magic. If you don't know how advanced energy workings operate, the methodologies of spirit summoning and conjuration, how a talismanic field operates, or what is needed to make an artifact fully empowered and capable of producing results by itself, then knowing how to *make* an artifact would be incomplete. I will present a short description of each of these kinds of magical operations and where a sigil or seal can make such an operation more successful.

ENERGY MODEL MAGICAL OPERATIONS

Raising magical energy is a simple process, but it can be applied in a very complex manner. It is a utilitarian technique of magic that is uniformly found in most basic systems of magic in the Western Mystery Tradition. However, it is a more modern system of magic because it uses techniques developed in the Eastern Mystery Tradition of yoga. Since we know that Empedocles used a system of elemental magic in ancient Greece and that it was part of the system of teachings of philosophy, especially the Pythagorean tradition, we can surmise that there must have been a method of energy magic practiced in antiquity. It was likely lost in the transition to Christianity, and the passage of time is the reason why it had to be reinvented in the modern age.

Energy magic is based on the two practices of breath control and bodily movement. Combined, they produce an expression and an experience of magic as materialized energy or power. I have also maintained in my writings and validated in my practices that there is a universal field of energy that can be tapped and integrated into a magical working through resonance and controlled ecstasy. To tap into the universal energy field, one only needs to trigger it through an intensive energy-raising exercise that borders on ecstasy. Obtaining this level of intensity in energy work will always be augmented by the universal energy field.

In order to be applied in a system of magic, the energy must be contained, shaped, compressed, imprinted, triggered, and then exteriorized. Combining breath and movement following specific symbolic qualifiers—such as the direction of the movement (deosil or widdershins), circumambulation, spiral walking, the manipulation of tools (dagger, sword, wand, or staff) and the drawing of devices (such as the pentagram or Rose Ankh Cross)—generates a field of energy to be used in a magical operation. Energy magic also uses the integral magical tool of the operator's will, but it is will energized by ecstasy.

More advanced techniques in energy magic make use of the points or nodes defined in a magic circle, such as the four cardinal directions (Watchtowers), the four points in-between the cardinal directions (which I call the Angles), and the three points in the center of the circle (called the nadir, mid-point, and zenith). These are the basic eleven points of the magic circle that I use to anchor the structures of magical energy that can be produced in this advanced methodology. One of the most basic structures is the cone of power, followed by more complex structures, such as the pyramid of power and the octagon. Circle structures, like the cardinal directions, hold the devices drawn, such as invoking pentagrams, but the energy is raised through a combination of movement and breath-control, which fills up these geometric structures with a field of energy. Vectoring of the spiral used to walk and push the power to the center of the circle will determine if the generated power is creative (deosil) or receptive (widdershins).

In the basic energy model, the walking widdershins spiral action proceeding from the center of the circle to the outer in three circuits is the primary method for exteriorizing the compressed energy into the mundane world. However, joining the Watchtowers together in a crossroads structure using the device of the Rose Ankh and a walking widdershins spiral action from the outer circle to the center in three circuits will generate an energy that I call a *receptive* or *negative vortex*. Laying down lines of force where the Watchtowers are joined laterally after being set with invoking pentagrams will produce a squared circle that is also a form of a *creative* or *positive energy-based vortex*.

The complex use of structures such as the pylon, where two devices are set to a zenith and nadir relationship and drawn together with an invoking spiral and set to the Watchtowers or Angles, will produce an intensified field of energy when it is raised within these structures. The octagon employs the qualification of the Watchtowers and Angles with differing attributes. In order to generate an elemental, for example, a magician performs a rite where an invoking pentagram of one element, set to the four Angles, is superimposed over the invoking pentagram of another element, set to the Watchtowers. Then, these eight nodes are drawn together through the zenith and nadir in the center of the circle to establish the structure of an elemental energy field once the energy of the elemental is summoned and raised. A magician can expand the number of circle nodes from eight to twelve or even sixteen, and they could use the mid-point (heart center) in the center of the circle as an anchor attaching the energy field to the body of the magician, incorporating the body's chakras as additional attribution points. The possibilities for the advanced energy model of magic are nearly endless.

While these various techniques are employed to raise and shape magical energy, it functions as the carrier in the information model of magic, and without defining the corresponding message and the line of transmission, the energy will not be able to effectively find the target and materialize the objective of the magical rite. While it might be possible to use the willpower of the magician alone to send the power to its target, developing a graphic symbol that represents the target and making it the link between subject and target is the proper—and more thorough—way to employ the energy model of magic. Once the energy has been raised and compressed into the center of the magic circle, it is imprinted using a consecrated sigil before being exteriorized and released into the mundane world. Thus, the raised energy is given a purpose and meaningful objective, raising it to the level of an empowered intelligence. As you can see, combining the energy model and information model greatly enhances the effectiveness of the magical working.

A standard pattern for producing the optimal ritual working that combines magical energy and symbolized information is the pyramid of power rite. This ritual working uses the combination of the invoking pentagram set to the four Watchtowers, the joining of the four nodes to erect a square within the magic circle, the defining of the zenith as the point where the four nodes join (to form a pyramid structure), and the walking deosil spiral from the periphery of the magic circle to the center of the circle to wind-up and compress the raised energy. Breath control (as cool breathing) and movement (as the walking spiral) are the mechanisms for raising the energy, but the structure of the pyramid captures and shapes the energy, and the invoking pentagram qualifies it. Once arriving at the center of the circle, the magician projects the image and symbolic meaning of the sigil into the energy, and then performs the reverse widdershins spiral walk from the center of the circle to the outer periphery, to release the power so that it might fulfill its purpose.

For the pyramid of power rite, the symbolic attribute of the raised energy combines the element energy of the invoking pentagram with the symbol of the ten attributes of godhead, as determined by the Qabalah or Pythagorean number symbology. There is the possibility of forty different energies (element plus number symbology), and I have named these forces the *forty Qualified Powers*. This symbolic attribute of qualified power merges with the sigil of the objective and link to the target to create an energized aspiration that is both highly effective and meaningful when released into the world. While the pyramid of power is a simple rite, it is most effective in quickly producing the magical working's desired results, so long as other elements of the working are in alignment and the corresponding mundane steps are also instituted.

Here is a step-by-step example of the ritual pattern of the pyramid of power ritual, executed in thirteen steps. It is assumed that the magician has performed divination into the background and nature of the magical objective and produced a charged and consecrated sigil representing that objective. It is also necessary to fully conceptualize the symbolic attribute of the qualified power to be used in the rite.

1. Proceed to the Eastern Watchtower and draw an invoking pentagram of the desired base element to the Watchtower using the dagger, projecting energy and one's breath into its center. Recite a simple prayer or exhortation that qualifies the Eastern cardinal direction.
2. Proceed to the Southern Watchtower and perform the same actions as performed to the East. Recite a prayer or exhortation appropriate to that direction.
3. Proceed to the Western Watchtower and perform the same actions as previously performed. Recite a prayer or exhortation appropriate to that direction.
4. Proceed to the Northern Watchtower and perform the same actions as previously performed. Recite a prayer or exhortation appropriate to that direction.
5. Proceed to the center of the circle and perform the same actions as previously performed, except that the invoking pentagram should be for creative spirit to the zenith. Recite a prayer or exhortation appropriate to that direction.
6. Return to the altar, deposit the dagger, and take up the sword.
7. Proceed to the East and with the sword, draw a line on the temple floor from the East to the South (deosil), and then from the South to the West, then to the North, continuing to the East. The four Watchtowers are drawn together into a square.

8. Return to the altar, deposit the sword, and take up the staff (or wand) with the right hand. Take up the consecrated sigil with the left and proceed to the East.
9. Face the South, extend the staff ahead of oneself, and then begin to walk around the circle three times in a spiral from the outer circle to the center, passing the East three times. While walking the spiral, use cool breathing to intensify the energy, and imagine that there is an ever-greater resistance as one proceeds to the center.
10. Once this step is completed, stand in the center of the circle facing North. Set the base of the staff at the nadir point, then draw the energy from the zenith down to the nadir through the staff, performing cool breathing and feeling the energy intensity at its highest level. Then, take the sigil and project its image into the energy arrayed around the staff, touch the sigil to the staff and internally summon the symbolic image and color of the qualified power, and quietly recite a prayer or exhortation. Place the sigil on the floor before the staff.
11. Holding the staff before oneself, turn to the North, then to the West, and begin to walk the spiral from the center of the magic circle around it, passing the North three times until the outer circle has been achieved. While walking this spiral, push and force the magic from the center of the circle, using a combination of cool breathing and bellows breath, toward the outer periphery of the circle. Imagine a great resistance making the circumambulation of the spiral more difficult with each step.
12. When reaching the outer circle at the point of the Northwest Angle, perform a short period of bellows breath, then project the energy outside of the magic circle in a great exhalation. In silence, internally recite a prayer or exhortation to direct the project's power to its ultimate purpose.
13. When these actions are completed and the rite is done, take the wand and draw sealing spirals to the four Watchtowers and the zenith. There is no need for banishment since the energy field was a positive vortex and cannot be banished.

SPIRIT MODEL MAGICAL OPERATIONS

What has passed down to us from the previous age regarding magical operations, outside of talismanic or celestial magic, is the invocation and evocation of spirits. Prior to the twentieth century, the popular consensus was that human beings did not have the power or authority to shape their destiny and the typical lot of human existence was locked into a way of life that had limited possibilities for advancement. If we consider what the status quo was like in late antiquity and continuing into the Middle Ages, then only a few members of the upper class could see themselves achieving the power of self-determination. The rest of the population served a master who determined their fate. Only the institution and traditions of the philosopher; the secret practices of magicians, sorcerers, and witches; and, later, the church, as well as those outside the law and civic jurisdictions, could say that they managed their own destinies. In such an environment that lasted from the Renaissance until the end of the nineteenth century, individuals who were not graced with wealth and status had little freedom to control their own destiny.

It is no wonder then that those who sought the powers of magic were also seeking to determine their own destiny. Yet, it was through the conjuration of spirits that one could apply the supernatural power vested in these entities to transform and change the limited opportunities plaguing those living in that world. In addition, it was assumed, especially in the Middle Ages, that one would have to achieve the grace of the Deity in order to command these spirits (as angels and demons) to comply with the magician's desires and designs. Therefore, anyone who aspired to wield these powers in this manner and assume the authority of God had to subject themselves to a rigorous purification process. It was assumed to be a very important and necessary stage to supposedly rid them of their sinful nature and achieve a level of piety that would allow them to command spirits. It was also believed that in order to command spirits, a magician needed an agent, guardian angel, or familiar spirit to help them, acting as an intercessor between the worlds of humanity and spirits.

Therefore, the first objective that a magician would seek to achieve was obtaining a spiritual intercessor. There were many formal methodologies for achieving this objective, and often they were less exalted and involved trafficking with fairies, earth spirits, and demons, which went against seeking the approbation of the Deity. There was a distinction between the literate cleric who used grimoires, the regimen of the church, and magically consecrated tools and vestments, and the illiterate peasant who used whatever was available to inspire the cunning fire or energy within them. A peasant would encounter a representative of the Other when seeking a way around their predicament of birth through unsanctioned pursuits, and a cleric would seek to wield the powers and prerogatives of the Deity to command the supernatural world.

From the literature of the grimoires, we have the prayers, invocations, talismans, seals, lamen, and various tools of the upper-class magician, and the methods they employed were also either documented or implied as being represented by five steps or stages in the work of spirit conjuration. These five steps were purification, invocation, constraining, binding, and releasing. This was the basic procedure followed to conjure demons and neutral spirits, but the constraining and binding were omitted and replaced with petitioning when it came to the conjuration of an angel. While the methods employed by the lower-class cunning folk were not typically written down until much later, we can get an idea (from numerous witch trials) that obtaining a familiar spirit was still the crucial first step, and then the use of summoning, constraining, binding, and releasing were a critical feature of their work. These five steps, used in some manner, were the basic pattern for spirit conjuration until modern times, and represent the regimen of the spirit-only model of magic promoted today.

My approach to the art of spirit conjuration is probably unique, but it uses ritual structures and energy fields to make the ritual process of invocation and evocation more tangible and objective. It also uses the symbolic artifices of the double gateway and the crossroads to establish the magical foundation for spirit conjuration.

Crossroads are used in the ritual structure of the negative or receptive vortex that generates the magnetic, contained energy that will hold and constrain the essence of the conjured spirit. A double gateway is used to represent the passage from the outer world into the inner world of spirits. The gate consists of the western entry into the underworld and the eastern exit into the outer world. Gateways are structured using a triangle, symbolizing the three-fold process of the cycles of entering and departing the underworld, where the spirit guide, guardian, and ordeal of transformation function in roles defined by whether one is entering or exiting this domain.

Using my methodology, an underworld is generated within the magic circle, where the crossroads and double gateway function as ritual mechanisms through which the descent into the underworld is realized. The operator is fully exposed to the conjured spirit residing in its domain, and it is only the agency of the activated familiar spirit (as the godhead within one) that mediates the powers and intelligence experienced within that domain. The invocation of a spirit in this type of magical working makes its realization and appearance much more powerful and intimate because it happens in the spirit's residence. A magician using my system of evocation comes face-to-face with the spirit called, as if they walked up to the spirit's home and knocked on door for a business call. It is imperative that the magician knows the character and reputation of the spirit that they are visiting.

Thus, I have found it useful to define the characteristics of the spirit in some symbolic manner, whether it is to use the seven planets qualified by one of the twelve zodiacal signs, or some other table of correspondences based on the Qabalah (Sephiroth, Pathways, Worlds), the planets, elements, zodiacal signs, and fixed stars, individually or in combination. I call this *invoking through a grid of correspondences*, and it has helped me to define the intelligence of the spirit that I am conjuring. I also use folklore and other occult literature to fully qualify and characterize the spirits that I seek to summon.

Early in my approach to spirit conjuration that I took from my studies merged an elemental energy generated through an octagon ritual working with a series of planetary invocations qualified by the signs of the zodiac. I joined an elemental spirit with a defined sevenfold planetary-based intelligence, and through the artifice of a vortex and gateway, created a multifaceted spiritual being with an energy body. I fortified this process by using sacraments, such as the consecrated wine and host from a mass, to aid the conjured spirit in gaining the flesh and blood of a full materialization. Later on, I used an array of correspondences to specifically qualify a spirit, replacing the seven-fold planetary intelligence with a symbolic correspondence. However, the final and most important artifact that I used was the charged and consecrated sigil, symbolically characterizing the essence of the spirit through the power of its name. In all of the workings using these techniques that I had developed, I used the sigil to initially summon a spirit and then compel it through offerings to give me a sign and seal to further extend and internalize our connection.

While the modern proponents of the spirit-only model of spirit conjuration—those who established this paradigm in the late 1990s—talked about the need for simplicity and the purity of their work, thus excluding more modern approaches to this magic, they had to use a sigil, seal, or sign to conjure a spirit. They had to know the name of the spirit, and they had to have some kind of characterization to give the process of summoning that spirit an independent realization. Even the most simplistic method of spirit conjuration relies on the information model of magic to give it form and identity. The use of sacrificial blood and flesh (where it is utilized), incense and devotions to the Deity, or the passion and willpower of the magician supplies the energy required for the carrier, and the sigil or seal functions as the message and link between subject and target. Without the use of the information model of magic, a conjuration will lack focus, definition, and will likely fail to produce any results. Sigils, seals, and marks provide the linguistic medium to the magic of spirit conjuration.

I have found that the process of developing and consecrating a spirit's sigil is a technique whereby that spirit is defined, characterized, and even imagined in the mind of the operator well before the rite of spirit conjuration is even performed. This is a significantly important step in the process of conjuration, although it is often omitted or simply stated as one of the preparation steps in that rite. As the first step of purification in an invocation or evocation rite, it is not specifically stated but is likely the most important preliminary step.

If we consider that the function of crafting the sigil or seal on parchment while imagining the characteristics of the target spirit—then consecrating that parchment with incense, a drop of sacramental wine, and the blowing of the breath of Spirit (pneuma) upon it—as a kind of mini-invocation, then it should be considered the most important preliminary step. These tasks set the parameters of the imagination and the expectation of results before the official conjuration is performed.

Consecrating a sigil or seal is the very first step that I take when considering performing a conjuration and, when combined with divination, makes the consecrated sigil or seal a bridge-fashioning technique between the spirit and me. It will certainly ensure that the conjuration will be successful, since it has already been initiated with this very first step of sigil consecration. It will also help to determine if the working should be done with the target spirit in focus. Spirit conjuration requires that the selected spirit in the working be capable and willing to take on and complete the magician's objective. Sometimes, divination can determine if the elected spirit is the right one to summon for a given objective.

The information model of magic is a critical part of spirit conjuration, and it belies the claim that a spirit-only model of magic will suffice for a successful operation. Since I do not follow this approach in my work with spirits, I add the energy model to my workings to intensify the overall impact and lend objective tangibility to the conjuration working. What I have discovered is using more than one model in a working makes for a better magical outcome, and this hybrid approach to working magic has served me extremely well over the decades of my magical pursuits.

A simple conjuration rite in my system of magic employs the Rose Ankh vortex as the base and the Western and Eastern gateways as the egress into the spiritual domain where the target spirit resides. The Rose Ankh is a purely archetypal feminine symbol, as opposed to the Rose Cross, which is archetypally masculine. The crossroads draw the widdershins walking spiral from the outer periphery of the magic circle into the center and project down through the nadir to fashion a kind of black hole, which will energetically define and hold the spirit once summoned. The Western Gateway deliberately opens up the spirit world as defined by the crossroads vortex and establishes the domain of the target spirit. One could further define an energy field within this vortex ritual structure to enhance and materialize the conjuration process, and the inclusion of sacramental applications (flesh and blood) would also help to solidify the body of the spirit.

Once these ritual structures are fully established, the operator can unveil the consecrated sigil or seal and perform the calling or summoning of the spirit in the center of this ritualized complex. The constraining of the spirit is where the operator uses consecrated tools, lamen, and talismans to urge the spirit to fully appear. Binding occurs when the operator makes offerings and produces a written agreement (also consecrated) so that the spirit will acknowledge and affirm that the objective will be successfully completed in the allotted time. Releasing is the same as giving the spirit a license to depart, but with understanding that the spirit will return when called upon, even without having to perform a formalized conjuration.

Purification and preparation for a conjuration will include a period of liturgical offerings, devotions, prayers, hymns, and the focusing of one's intention on the objective of the rite. I will typically spend two weeks doing this kind of work. It will also be the time when the sigil or seal is crafted and consecrated, the timing of the rite determined, any auspices for the elected date and time examined, and divination performed on the working itself, as well as the all-important aftermath. Prior to the hour of the working, I will clean and order the working temple, ensuring that it is fully supplied with everything required, and then perform the important self-ablutions, taking a magical bath, anointing oneself, and donning clean vestments. In my workings, I have added the rites of the Mass and the Benediction to generate the required sacraments and to empower the temple, sacralizing it, and making it a fit place to conjure spirits. These steps often will start producing materialized results even before the conjuration rite is performed, and that will certainly be a predictor for a successful working.

Here is the pattern that I would use to perform a simple conjuration for a spirit. While different classes of spirits require different approaches to this kind of rite (I have a number of different rituals depending on the spirit that I aim to conjure), I can define this process in a simple manner, requiring just a set of steps to accomplish the objective: a full manifestation of a spirit. I must first fully define the preparatory steps as I would perform them, since these steps set the stage for a successful conjuration.

PREPARATION STEPS

1. Perform a period (two weeks or more) of liturgical workings to inaugurate the process of doing a conjuration. This would include accomplishing daily meditation sessions; making weekly devotions to your pantheon of Deities; giving offerings of food and drink, prayer, and hymns of praise; executing a godhead assumption and communion with one's primary Deity; and requesting assistance in the planned working.
2. Design, develop, and craft the sigil or seal for the target spirit. Perform a consecration rite to charge and sacralize the parchment sigil or seal. Research the image and characteristics of the spirit and perform probing divination sessions on the spirit using its consecrated sigil as the link. Journal any occurrences that seem significant. Prior to the working, the consecrated sigil or seal should be kept in a pouch or covered by a dark cloth.
3. Analyze and examine the auspices of the date and time set for the conjuration. This can be a simple process of observing the lunar phases and solar season or a more detailed examination of the astrological transits occurring during the day and the hour of the working. Ensure that the date and time elected are convenient and auspicious.

4. On the day of the working, observe the passage of the Sun through the four stations and perform meditation sessions to help promote the best mind state possible for the working. Take a long and relaxing herbal bath, anoint oneself (forehead, throat, heart, and left and right shoulders), and then dress in the prepared vestments and adorn oneself with appropriate jewelry.
5. Perform a Mass rite and a Benediction rite as preparation for the work. These ceremonies should be performed in a consecrated circle. While doing these rites, perform a simple rite to assume one's godhead. Additionally, a small altar or table is placed in the center of the circle off to the left side, and a cup of sacramental wine and a dish of a host fragment are placed on it, along with a lit stick of incense. Place the consecrated pact or petition on the central altar, as well as a pair of dice.

CONJURATION RITE

1. Take the wand and proceed to the Northern Watchtower. Draw a Rose Ankh device into the Watchtower and project a magnetic energy into it using the cool breath technique. Then, drawing a line with the wand from the North, walk to the West.
2. Proceed to the Western Watchtower. Perform the same operation as in the North, then, using the wand, draw a line from the West to the South.
3. Proceed to the Southern Watchtower. Perform the same operation as in the West, then, using the wand, draw a line from the South to the East.
4. Proceed to the Eastern Watchtower. Perform the same operation, then, using the wand, draw a line from the East to the North.

Foundational Rites Used in the Notary Art

5. Return to the altar, deposit the wand, and pick up the sword.
6. Proceed to the Northern Watchtower and, using the sword, draw a line from the Rose Ankh suspended there to the center of the magic circle at the point of the nadir.
7. Proceed to the Western Watchtower and with the sword, perform the same operation.
8. Proceed to the Southern Watchtower and perform the same operation.
9. Proceed to the Eastern Watchtower and perform the same operation.
10. Return to the altar and exchange the sword for the staff.
11. Proceed to the Northern Watchtower. Turn to face the West and begin to circumambulate the magic circle, walking an inward spiral and passing the North three times to the center of the circle. Hold the staff forward from one's body and project a dark energy, using cool breathing, from the outer circle into the center. Upon arriving in the center of the circle, set the base of the staff on the nadir point and project energy through and below that point, kneeling before it. The vortex is set.
12. Return to the altar and replace the staff.
13. Proceed to the Eastern Watchtower and turn to face the West.
14. Draw an invoking spiral with the hand to the Southeast Angle (left) and visualize the guide who assists one in the passage.
15. Draw an invoking spiral with the hand to the Northeast Angle (right) and visualize the guardian who one must overcome to proceed.
16. Draw an invoking spiral with the hand to the West (front) and visualize the ordeal of transformation (shattering and reintegration).

17. Draw lines of force with the hands from the Southeast to the West, from the West to the Northeast, and from the Northeast to the Southeast. The triangle gateway is established.
18. Proceed slowly forward toward the West with hands before oneself as if groping for the way in the darkness. When arriving before the Western Watchtower, make the sign of the enterer (opening the veil), proceed forward one step, and turn to face the East. Draw the power of the gateway down through one's body, imagining a cascading ray of sparkling golden light.
19. Proceed slowly forward, imagining oneself descending a flight of stairs into a basement-like underworld. Turn to face the West, then sit and perform a brief meditation. The underworld domain of spirits has been reached.
20. Proceed to the altar. Take up the wand in the right hand and unveil the consecrated sigil or seal and take it with the left hand, along with the invocation script.
21. Proceed to the center of the circle. Sit down and assume a meditation stance. Perform a deep trance activating the previous godhead assumption. Return to a light trance state, then read the prepared invocation three times, each more emotional and emphatic than the previous. Wave the wand to the West, performing three invoking spirals to emphasize the invocation.
22. Call and summon the spirit to appear. Entice it with the offerings of sacrament and incense placed on the small central altar. When the spirit finally appears, acknowledge that it is present. If you do not have the ability to converse, make use of the dice for yes (even numbers) or no (odd numbers) questions; otherwise, proceed to engage in a dialogue with the spirit.
23. Take up the pact with the objective clearly written on it, along with the expected time period for its completion. Place the consecrated sigil or seal upon the pact or petition and replace it on the central altar.

Offer the consecrated wine and host to the spirit for its consumption and promise to renew that offering once the objective has been met. Present it to the spirit.
24. Stand, bow before the central altar, thank the spirit for its visit, and give it license to depart with the stipulation that future callings can be employed.
25. Return to the altar and replace the wand.
26. Proceed to the Western Watchtower, make the sign of the closing portal (closing the veil), and then turn to face the East.
27. Draw an invoking spiral with the hand to the Northwest Angle (left) and visualize the guide who assists one in the exit.
28. Draw an invoking spiral with the hand to the Southwest Angle (right) and visualize the guardian who one must overcome to exit.
29. Draw an invoking spiral with the hand to the East (front) and visualize the ordeal of translation (encapsulating the acquired wisdom through art).
30. Draw lines of force with one's hands from the Northwest to the East, and from the East to the Southwest, and from the Southwest to the Northwest. The triangle gateway is established.
31. Proceed slowly forward toward the East, with hands before one, as if groping for the way out of the darkness. When arriving before the Eastern Watchtower, make the sign of the enterer (opening the veil), proceed forward one step, and turn to face the West. Draw the power of the gateway down through one's body, imagining a cascading ray of sparkling golden light.
32. Proceed slowly forward, imagining one ascending a flight of stairs into a brilliant dawning day. Turn to face the East, then sit and perform a brief meditation. The outer world of humanity has been achieved.
33. Stand and perform the closing portal sign to the East, then draw sealing spirals to the four Watchtowers. The rite is ended.

PSYCHOLOGICAL AND TEMPORAL MODEL MAGICAL OPERATIONS

Combining the psychological and temporal models produces a system of magic named *celestial* or *talismanic magic*. A pure planetary magical working only requires invoking the planetary spirit during a date and time considered most auspicious for such a working. A planetary intelligence, given the name and qualities of a spirit, still functions within the parameters of the planetary archetype, so there is no difference between the spirit, its character, and the astrological qualities it represents. Planetary intelligences are attributes of archetypal qualities and characteristics and therefore represent aspects of the mind. The timeliness of such an operation, and the associated astrological auspices, symbolize the background and potentialities associated with that moment.

However, I have found that using just these two components does not satisfy the requirements for what I have defined as the talismanic equation. That requires an energy, a hierarchy of spirits, godheads, and the use of sigils and seals to complete it. It would seem that a pure and simple approach to talismanic magic is not as effective as it could be by including both energy and spirits to this process. This is also true with nearly every kind of magic, since in my experience, they all seem to work better when the information model of magic is included.

In my early days of working magic, I found that the simple combination of planet and element produced a matrix of twenty-eight qualities that combined the intelligence of a planetary archetype with the energized base of an element. That combination turned out to be very powerful indeed, and, in fact, it became the basis of what I came to define as talismanic magic. The only system of magic that I discovered where such a combination of planet and element was used was the Enochian system of magic. There are twenty-four spirits named the Seniors who reside in a matrix of six planets (Saturn, Jupiter, Mars, Venus, Mercury, Luna) and four elements (Air, Water, Earth, Fire), and adding in the four spirit kings of the Sun, produces the twenty-eight planetary spirits of the four Enochian Watchtowers, or as I call them, talismanic elementals. It seemed obvious to me that this should be the foundation of talismanic magic, but it appears that my approach is too untraditional for some.

Over the years, I have found that these twenty-eight talismanic elementals can also be matched with the twenty-eight lunar mansions, although there are a few outliers. That meant that my talismanic elementals were also represented astrologically as the lunar mansions, which gave them a powerful temporal assignment. What I discovered was that one needed an elemental energy field joined with a planet to produce the talismanic field that could be used to project and charge a talismanic artifact. Whether that element was provided by an invoking pentagram or through the qualities of an associated zodiacal sign, a proper talisman required both an archetypal intelligence and an elemental energy field. This is true for using the thirty-six decans in talismanic workings (a zodiacal sign and a decan ruling planet) or the forty-eight septans (a zodiacal sign, ruling planet, and element zodiacal sub-section), a structure that I created through my own research and experimentation.

Talismanic magic, as I have defined it, requires an element and a planet, but also must be performed at the right time. The auspices of a moment where talismans are created requires a greater rigor than any other system of magic. Not only must the planetary transits, phases of the Moon, solar position, and season be considered as important criteria, but also the planetary day, hours, and weather must be considered when one is contemplating a talismanic working. Even one's natal chart might be consulted to find the most auspicious and significant time to perform the working.

The rationale for such a deep astrological analysis is that the talismanic artifact holds an indelible imprint of the time of its creation, and that imprint will profoundly affect the magic that it will generate. Unlike any other form of magic, talismans after they are charged and incubated operate around the clock, every day, perpetually. Unless a talisman is destroyed, it will continue to operate as long as the wielder keeps some kind of conscious link with it. A talisman that is charged and set with either poor or malefic auspices will function more like an automated curse than a progressive benefactor. Fully vetting the auspices of a talisman is a critical exercise to be implemented before performing the rite to produce it.

The information model of magic does not appear to be a factor in talismanic magic at first glance. Certainly, one could perform talismanic magic effectively without recourse to the information model, but using it helps to focus, refine, and set or reset the programmed function of the talisman. When I produce a talismanic artifact, I use a sigil inked on a piece of parchment and consecrated to symbolically express the objective to which I am employing the talisman, just as if I were producing a sigil for an energy working. I also use sigils and seals to define the hierarchy of spirits associated with the talismanic field; I can even employ these various sigils in the design and crafting of the metallic talismanic artifact. When I want to shift the focus of the talisman to another related objective, I can use a newly created and consecrated sigil to make it happen, using it as a means to magically communicate with the talisman.

Sigils can be used to set the programming for a talisman within the parameters of the talismanic field and auspices established when it was produced, and they can also be used to communicate and reset the programming whenever required. I also use them to transfer a talisman that I charged and created to a client. Through the use of a sigil, I could theoretically diminish or enhance the power of talisman, like turning the volume down or up on an audio device, or even shut it off so the talisman would become dormant. The utility of a charged and consecrated sigil is nearly endless when applied to a talisman, although it is constrained by the characteristics that were built into the talisman when it was created. To apply a consecrated sigil to a talisman, all one needs to do is place the talisman in contact with the sigil for a period of twenty-four hours. I usually place a cloth over both the talisman and the sigil to ensure proper incubation for that period.

Unlike the last two model methods of magic, I won't get into the specifics of the patterns used and show where the sigils and seals can be used in a talismanic working. There are too many steps to cover, and I have a book already in print that should cover the specifics of incorporating the information model of magic into the combined psychological and temporal models.[29] However, even in talismanic magic, the use of sigils and seals play an important role in the imprinting, focusing, and directing the talismanic field.

Integrating the notary art into standard magical workings represents the most basic function to expanding the capabilities of those operations. I have given very specific examples showing how the information model of magic not only fits into other models of magic seamlessly, but also that the reason for that perfect fit is because it is a system of magic by itself. Building it into one's practical magical methodologies and workings completes those systems, especially for the models of energy and spirit. Using breath control and trance techniques, the notary art comes alive, and through the artifice of sacred space, it is given a sacralized foundation. These two techniques, breath-control and trance, can and should become integral to the notary art, since every action that makes symbolic forms of graphic representation should be seen as a magical act, whether utilized in other magical workings or by itself.

Perceived in the correct altered state of consciousness, symbolic representations become a simulacrum of what they represent, seeming to appear as the very thing that they characterize. The aphorism that thought becomes form and form becomes thought symbolizes the mid-point between worlds that the notary art seeks to bridge. Still, we have only shown how the notary art can be used in three different models. We should now briefly examine the full spectrum of magic that the information model spans.

---

[29] Frater Barrabbas, *Talismanic Magic for Witches* (Llewellyn Publications, 2023).

CHAPTER TEN

USING THE NOTARY ART IN MAGICAL RITES

WE HAVE NOW FULLY COVERED the details about crafting various kinds of sigils names, seals, sigil objectives, godhead signatures, magical alphabets, magical formulas, and magical notae. Each of these comprises a magical discipline unto itself, and although briefly covered in this book, they represent the whole collective of the various types of notary magic. We have also discussed how to build these various artifacts, and how to consecrate and charge them. It is up to you to study and practice these techniques, and to develop the lore I have written here so that you can become a master at producing any of these kinds of artifacts whenever you might need to use them.

Additionally, we examined the various systems of magic that employ sigils and seals in the previous chapter and defined in specific detail how the methods of the information model of magic can make other models more precise, focused, and empowered. Without having a sigil or seal, spirit conjuration would certainly not be very effective, and the development of the advanced energy model would be groundless without a sigil to accurately define and direct the energy of a working. However, we should examine how these ritual workings are impacted by sigils, seals, signatures, and notae in a more general manner, showing how this art form is integral to all magical workings and functions as a system of magic itself. I will also tie these different models of magic to books that I have already published, which can be used to develop these systems of magic in greater detail.

This, of course, brings us to our final overall analysis and exposition: how to employ these potent artifacts in the magic that you are already performing, and how to use them in a form of magic where the artifact alone is wielded. You will find that there are some basic practices using various models of magic where employing a consecrated artifact can make the difference between a successful outcome and failure. We will examine the full spectrum of possible uses for the notary art, but only briefly outline them here.

Sigils help you to develop the magical link between your aspirations and desires and the object of that passionate desire, helping you both formulate and reduce those aspirations and desires to that one thing. The basic secret to successful magic is that the object of that magic is refined, honed down, and stripped of vagaries or opposing cross-purposes so that the final result is a clearly defined target with associated mundane steps. Putting an initial desire and objective through that process will eliminate redundancies and duplications, simplifying something that might have multiple objectives.[30] Of course, different types of magic will require a more rigorous process of reduction and clarification. Certainly, invoking or evoking a spirit is a one-pointed objective, but the spirit must also be capable of performing the operator's request, and sometimes developing a sigil and a mark or signature needs to incorporate further study to ensure that the spirit is the appropriate entity to perform a task. So, different models or types of magic require different types of notary artifacts, and they employ them in different ways.

There are six basic models of magic that can be employed by a magician, although most systems of magic represent a combination of these models. There is the energy model, the

---

[30] Frater Barrabbas, *Elemental Powers for Witches* (Llewellyn Publications, 2021) pp. 187–194. The whole chapter is an excellent discussion of how to reduce an objective down to that one thing, and why it is important to do that.

spirit model, the psychological and temporal models (used together), the chaos or stochastic model, and the information model of magic. Each of these models of magic will rely on the use of different types of notary artifacts and will employ them in distinct manner. Let's examine each one of these hypothetical models and discuss how notary artifacts can make them much more successful.

IMPRINTING AND DIRECTING RAISED ENERGY FIELDS

The energy model of magic is all about raising energy, focusing and targeting it, and then releasing it so that it can empower an objective, bending the associated probabilities for an outcome and making the potential possibility an actuality. Two factors must be introduced in magic that uses energy fields, or the end result will produce either nothing or something undesired. These two factors are establishing and defining the magical link and imprinting the energy field with a purpose and direction. An energy spell that does not have a well-defined link will fail to be transmitted to the objective of the magic and the inherent message will be vague or non-existent. Passion by itself, although an excellent source of magical energy, cannot accomplish a premeditated goal with any degree of accuracy or consistency.

What this means is that energy fields alone will not be sufficient to achieve a successful magical outcome on a consistent basis without incorporating features of the information model of magic. If you are seeking to affect some possibility through the use of energy-based magic, then unless you are directly absorbing that energy or applying it directly to someone or something to charge it, you will have very inconsistent results without employing a magical link. I know this to be a fact because I performed a lot of failed energy-based magic in my years as a novice because I did not know how to employ a magical link.

Mastering the art of creating sigils that encapsulate the desires and objective of a magical working and then applying them to imprint the energy fields prior to releasing them is the perfect mechanism for ensuring a successful outcome. A sigil of aspiration is a graphic symbol that represents the magic's objective, and when it is consecrated and charged, the very first step in a magical working involving energy fields has already been accomplished.

You can think of the charged sigil of aspiration as the key to the working's successful outcome. This is because you carefully defined, reduced, condensed, and symbolically established the focus for the working on one single objective. Correspondingly, you have also defined the mundane steps required to accompany the sigil of aspiration and assist in its successful achievement. Raising the energy, imprinting it, and then exteriorizing it are the final steps to a process that began with the process to develop a sigil of aspiration.

My favorite use of sigils of aspiration in the energy model of magic is to employ them when performing elemental magic with the sixteen elementals or working with the forty qualified powers. I believe that the marriage of sigil magic with energy field magic makes for a perfect magical working, and I have found that the results are often consistent and successful.

In my book *Elemental Powers for Witches,* I showed how to merge the energy model of magic with the information model to generate powerful energy fields that help to fully realize a short-term goal.[31] This is a complete and comprehensive approach to this kind of magic, and I feel that it will assist you in developing this kind of magic so that you can readily make use of it whenever needed.

In that book, I covered not only how to conjure elemental and qualified elemental spirits, but also how to generate magical energy and develop sigils of aspiration to construct magical links and imprint and direct energy fields. It is comprehensive work that contains everything that you need to know to perform this kind of magic.

---

31 Frater Barrabbas, *Elemental Powers for Witches* (Llewellyn Publications, 2021) pp. 121–131, 146–148.

SYMBOLIC NAMING FOR INVOKED OR EVOKED SPIRITS

Many traditions of magic engage in conjuring spirits into some degree of manifestation to direct them to engage and fulfill a material, mental, or spiritual objective. Whether the spirits are angels, demons, or neutral Earth or Air spirits, the same approach to identifying them is required in order for the working to be successful. This is the spirit model of magic, and there are some traditions in that type of magic that promote the idea that this model is the only true model of magic. Of course, that is an erroneous presumption, especially when the most important required artifact used in this kind of working is the sigil, seal, mark, or signature of the spirit.

As we have already discussed this concept in Part I of this book and the previous chapter, using a consecrated and charged sigil or seal in a ritual of invocation or evocation is a critical piece of notary art that is employed to ensure a successful outcome of this kind of magic. You need to know the name of a spirit in order to call it, and you then need to fashion that name into a symbolic graphic form so that it can communicate its identity and essence between the material and spiritual worlds. If this were not so, then there wouldn't be any seals and sigils found in the various grimoires and textbooks to aid in the conjuration of spirits.

Whether or not such sigils and seals were used by magicians, Witches, and sorcerers in antiquity is a good question, but that question was succinctly answered by the plethora of such artifacts found in the *Greek Magical Papyri* (*PGM*) that dates from the second and third century CE. It would seem based on this text that these sigils, seals, and unusual marks, along with the barbarous words of evocation, were very much a part of the techniques of magic in antiquity. The notary art of magic has a very long, varied, and distinguished history, and it has a place in modern magic as well.

Needless to say, the sigil or seal, consecrated and charged, is the key to successfully conjuring a spirit. However, the magical action of conjuring a spirit is only the first step that a magician must perform to work this kind of magic. They must not only conjure the spirit but also give it a direction and a purpose, to establish, as it were, an agreement or pact for it to fulfill. Spirit conjuration is actually a two-step process, since once the spirit is manifested in some form, then the magician must establish the goal or objective for it to achieve as part of the agreement.

I have found that such a pact or agreement should be written down on paper, and if it were to be used to craft a sigil or aspiration, then that would be, in my opinion, an optimal strategy. Therefore, you can use the notary art to fashion a sigil, seal, mark, or signature, and you can also use the notary art to craft a sigil of aspiration that will powerfully link a spirit and an objective.

Similar to the art of using the energy model of magic, my book, *Spirit Conjuring for Witches*, covers the art and methodology for spirit conjuration, invocation, and evocation in a comprehensive manner. This book covers all of the techniques and methods that you would need to translate a Witchcraft or Pagan type of magic to performing ritual conjuration of spirits. It would give such folk access to the grimoires that are all the rage in the ceremonial crowd as well as allow them to approach such books armed with a magical technology that makes them easy to access and understand. Such traditional lore serves for the practicing Witch or Pagan as adjuncts to the magical toolkit that they already possess.

In this book, I have defined the notary art for the purpose of ritually conjuring spirits; I also cover this topic in my *Spirit Conjuring for Witches* book, although perhaps not as singularly.[32] Everything that you need to perform invocations and evocations can be found in that book, including crafting sigils and communicating with spirits. Still, this book has given you the impetus to acquire and study that book, and by that action, you will only grow and expand your knowledge and experience of the notary art of sigil and seal construction.

---

32 Frater Barrabbas, *Spirit Conjuring for Witches* (Llewellyn Publications, 2017) pp. 114–123.

BUILDING A TEMPORAL LINK AND DIRECTING TALISMANS

Talismanic magic uses a combination of planetary attributes and elemental energy to generate a talismanic field that continuously impacts the material world in accordance with the magical intention and objective of the magician. It is probably the most powerful magic that a magician can employ simply because the talismanic field is continuously in operation. It is also true that the magician must use a great deal of care and thoroughly research their own astrological natal chart to ensure that the talismanic field will produce the kind of impact and effect that will produce the desired results.

The objective of this magic is implied by the quality and attribution of the specific talismanic field the magician has chosen to wield. The associated planetary intelligence, the empowered element field, and the auspices of when this magic is deployed collectively determine the magical objective. If that objective has cross-purposes with either the natal chart attributes of the magician or the timing when this work was performed, then it will be not only less effective, but it might produce outcomes that were completely undesired.

This kind of magic uses two kinds of links to make it effective and the outcome successful. These two links are the objective of the work, made explicit through the artifice of a sigil of aspiration, and the temporal link, which includes the attributes of the talismanic field and the moment in time when it was deployed. A sigil of aspiration is not typically discussed in the context of talismanic magic, but it can be used to direct the already charged and infused talismanic artifact to achieve a specific objective. In a word, a sigil of aspiration is the perfect mechanism for talking or communicating with a talisman once it is made.

The other symbolic link is the temporal link that characterizes a talisman once it is fully activated. A temporal link is a snapshot of the time and location that a magical event occurred. You don't need to incorporate a temporal link when using the spirit or energy models, but the temporal model of magic requires it. Not only does the temporal link establish the event of talismanic magic, but it also has a determinative effect on the possessor's destiny. A temporal link consists of two basic components. These are to establish a temporal signature that can be accessible between the worlds of matter and spirit, and to mark a milestone event and give it a powerful emphasis in the current space-time continuum of the talisman's possessor. A temporal link also establishes a timeline for when the expected objective should be achieved.

A temporal link should contain the seasonal, diurnal solar aspects along with the specific phase and lunation type for the Moon. These two elements combined will produce a symbolic expression of time. The location is defined as the exact place where the talismanic magic is performed to produce the artifact. In general, a temporal link consists of the following six elements:

1. Solar Hour as Planetary Hour and Solar Day as Planetary Day
2. Sun in Zodiacal Sign: in relation to nearest Equinox or Solstice
3. Moon in Zodiacal Sign: seasonal Moon in relation to the four phases
4. Lunation Type: eight phases of the Moon
5. Geological Matrix: latitude, longitude, altitude, and even weather conditions
6. Internal Domain of the Practitioner: natal zodiacal chart and transit chart

Only the first four of these six points are the most critical, used to determine the temporal link. In order to cause material manifestations and alterations, the magician should first determine the attributes of the talismanic field and its overall effects on the possessor; the second step is to determine the temporal signature.[33]

---

33 Frater Barrabbas, *Talismanic Magic for Witches* (Llewellyn Publications, 2023) pp. 168–169. Context for the temporal link associated with talismanic magic.

While a temporal link would not necessarily be considered an attribute of the notary art, the act of forging the metallic talisman artifact etched with the sigils of the spiritual hierarchy and the seal of an Olympian spirit, along with any other qualifying sigils of aspiration, would very much be a part of the notary art. Additionally, astronomy and astrology would be considered adjuncts to the notary art, as would all forms of divination. Markings or etchings on a metallic talisman artifact might not be required or considered critical, but there is a corresponding parchment sigil that is used to help imprint the talismanic field, thus also making this operation very much a part of the notary art.

Similarly with the other two models of magic, I have published a book titled *Talismanic Magic for Witches* that thoroughly covers the methodologies of making metallic talisman artifacts. You are invited to explore this work if you would like to know more about talismanic magic and will also find that the notary art is well-represented in this book as an important tool to the creation of a talisman.

DEITY PLACEHOLDERS AND NAMING ANIMATED STATUES OR PICTURES

I previously discussed that you could use a magical alphabet to translate names into graphically empowered labels to use as name tags for the statues or images of Deities and spirits that are typically arrayed on a shrine altar. These are the kind of entities that have a special place in the life and practice of a Witch, Pagan, or ritual magician. What I did not state was that these very same labels could be used as placeholders for these same beings.

If these translated labels are consecrated consecutively three times, then they can be considered representations for the entities that they identify in the magical alphabet. Such an artifact would be used to label an animated statue, symbolic sculpture, magic stone, or a picture to affix an identity to that object and tie it to the ultimate spiritual essence of that being. This kind of magic would be correctly assigned to a form of theurgy, since it would fully and accurately define a spiritual being in a material manner to be able to communicate and emanate its intelligence and authorities into the material world and in the presence of those who worship it. This is the basic method for employing this kind of magical name notary art, it is to specifically identify a spiritual being associated with an animated statue, marker, or picture, and make a bridge or doorway to it to travel to this world.

However, this kind of magical artifact is also portable, especially if the name is written on a piece of parchment or a piece of jewelry. You can wear this kind of artifact on your person, hidden by clothes, or placed in a pocket, wallet, or purse, which will ensure that the spiritual represented by the artifact will be with you wherever you are. Doing this simple thing will help to empower and protect you with the powers and authorities of that entity, and it also makes a godhead assumption easier and more direct if the name on that artifact happens to be the name of the deity to which you are bonded. Wearing such an artifact on your person would certainly cover you with spiritual grace and protect and energize you as you go through your daily life. It makes the phrase "Go with God" seem much more appropriate, possible, and even actualized.

Of course, using magical labels to act as a doorway for spiritual entities would require that you have animated markers, statues, or pictures available for this kind of magic. As an adjunct to the theurgy of statue animation, it requires that such an artifact representing the Deity be made available, and that technology cannot be discussed in this work.

If you want to fully understand how to animate a statue, picture, or representational marker, then I have another book for you to consider in the *For Witches* series of books. In my book *Sacramental Theurgy for Witches*, I have dedicated an entire chapter to the art and methodology of statue animation.[34] It, of course, uses sacramental magic, but it also employs talismanic magic. In short, I have deduced that the ancient art of statue animation can be readily replicated if the operator places a talismanic field upon the object that is to house the essence of the Godhead.

---

34   Frater Barrabbas, *Sacramental Theurgy for Witches* (Crossed Crow Books, 2024) pp. 109–113.

Once a talismanic field is deployed, then the operator performs a drawing down rite on the statue, and attributes of the Deity are retained in the perpetual energies and intelligent field of the talisman. I have performed this operation several times and it has always worked quite effectively. Once you have an animated statue, then you can apply to it the artifact of the magical name of that entity, which will complete the process and make a doorway between the world of the spirits and our material world.

INFORMATION MAGICAL MODEL: USING CONSECRATED SIGILS AND NOTAE ALONE

The information model of magic establishes a link between the subject and the target using the mechanisms of information theory to identify the devices of the message, carrier, and the line of transmission, ensuring that magic always has a directive to follow to achieve a defined objective. However, unlike the other models of magic, the information model magic can stand by itself and does not require any other model's attributes to function. With perhaps the exception of energy, a magical link can function by itself. The energy attribute comes from the act of activating the artifact, so there is no requirement for an energy field such as what is used in the energy model of magic.

Some chaos magicians lionized this model of magic and proposed that it was the only true model. Once again, such a claim should be seen as absurd in its merit because so many of the models are tightly integrated together and cannot be seen as separate methodologies. I would agree with the perspective that everything is tied together, but there are some attributes of the information model of magic that make it appear to be separate and distinct from all of the other models of magic. This is because some of the techniques of sigil magic can be performed without any use of other techniques or magical methods.

Of all of the different kinds of notary artifacts, the ones that could be used without any other type of magic would be the sigils of aspiration, the alphabet of desire sigils, and the notae, which represent the synthesis of words, geometric forms, and even sigils of spirit names or aspirations. Sigils of aspiration are unique in that they can be used alone, without any other magical methods. Once activated, they can be used to perform a magical operation through the artifice of meditation and deep trance states. There is no need for a magical temple, sacred space, tools, or any other accoutrements other than the sigil and the tools to make and consecrate it. It is portable and can be employed whenever needed, so there is no need to determine the temporal link.

Based on the information theory as applied to magic, establishing any kind of link creates a line of transmission between the subject and the object of a magical working. That line of transmission functions as a doorway between worlds, bridging the material and spiritual worlds, and the worlds of individual consciousness and the collective consciousness of a culture. While I don't subscribe to the idea of an unconscious mind being more than a part of the autonomous functions of the body and the foundation of emotional and perceptual sensations, others believe that sigils of aspiration impact this unconscious mind. Such an unconscious mind has a collective and an individual dimension, so pushing a sigil into the unconscious mind is believed to make it travel to its destination.

This belief is why most systems of sigil magic require the operator to disengage their focus and then quickly forget what they have put into motion, thus releasing the power of the sigil into the unconscious mind. I believe that this intense connection and release is in the nature of magic itself and relates to the ancient art of cord magic: to constrain, bind and release. It should be noted that if the line of transmission is kept open, such as when connecting to deities or spiritual agencies, then the process of releasing should occur over a greater period of time. It is important to effectively manage the doorway that this kind of magic produces and to not leave doors open or forget to shut them, allowing for unwanted energies and entities to gain entry and access to you. Closing the doorway may sometimes involve burning a sigil if it is perishable.

Once a sigil of aspiration or a nota has been crafted, consecrated, and charged, using that artifact is a very simple process. Until the operator becomes accustomed to this kind of magical work, or if they are working with a newly fashioned artifact, it is prudent to experiment with the artifact to fully understand and realize its capabilities.

Key states of consciousness to unlock the sigil or nota are the basic state of deep meditation, followed by deep trance. You should be seated in a comfortable asana on a cushion or chair and, holding the sigil in your dominant hand, enter into the deeper states of meditation and trance. It is important to gain a strong trance state, but not too strong. You will want to maintain a certain amount of conscious volition so that you can observe the effects and the impact of the sigil or nota.

If you have already experimented with the sigil and are familiar with its effect, then you can enter into a trance state, with eyes closed and inwardly focused, and begin to project the energies and symbolic construct of the sigil into the domain of spirit to push the symbolized message to the target. You can soundlessly chant the sigil mantra in your mind or just use vernacular language to project your will through the sigil and towards the target. You can visualize the events that you desire occurring, and also mentally visualizing the mundane steps that you will take to help make this objective realized. This is how you would use a sigil of aspiration to make a desired outcome fully realized. You are using your will, but you are employing the encapsulated graphic symbol to communicate your desire through the collective consciousness to impact your desired objective.

Using a nota requires a somewhat different approach. You will perform the meditation and trance induction, but you will focus your attention on the design of the nota, reciting the words of power and exhortations that are incorporated into it. If there are spirit names associated with it, then you will call and summon them. Once you sense the nota opening up, becoming like an active window to another world, and the associated spirits responding to your requests, then you can state your request and the objective of your magic, asking for this favor or boon to be revealed and awarded to you.

Magic using a nota is typically for obtaining of some kind of internalized mental process or the transmission of lore, ideas, and insights. It is not typically used to cause material objectives to be met, although one could do this in an oblique manner if the knowledge that is sought would help in obtaining material rewards. Nota can be used to bring spiritual realizations through the operator and into the world, so in this manner, it functions as a kind of theurgic working.

Once the operator has completed the working and there appears to be nothing further to be experienced, they will return to full consciousness and release their focus on the sigil or nota. The operator should then perform a grounding exercise and proceed in doing other mundane things to fully disengage with the magic that has been performed. The magic will require a period of incubation, especially if a nota has been used (but that is also true for a sigil of aspiration). It is prudent that the operator makes certain that any thoughts about the magical work just completed are forgotten for a period of time, allowing the powers, authorities, and intelligences to do their work without interference.

Sigil magic using a sigil of aspiration can also be collected and then burned after forty-eight hours if it has been written onto perishable surfaces, such as parchment. I typically do not make my sigils of aspiration using anything other than parchment, since I make and use them as a one-time magical process. This is not the way a nota is handled, of course, because it is typically drawn on imperishable surfaces such as wood or metal. With a nota, I either cover it up with a cloth or put it into a folder or box and store it in a drawer.

As you can see, working with a sigil of aspiration or a nota is a simple process once the artifact is created, consecrated, and charged. It requires the ability to assume a deep trance state without debilitating the functionality of the operator. It is important to use the concept magical ligature when employing these kinds of artifacts so that the constraining, binding, and releasing are the important stages of this process of magic. I have performed many workings using these methods and have found them mostly successful.

At times, it is important to work forms of divination alongside any kind of sigil magic so that the operator can understand the nature of the objective and observe its effects. A divination reading used to analyze the effects of a magical operation using sigils of aspiration should be performed a few weeks after the working is completed, so that the operator doesn't interfere with the magical process. I would recommend waiting for a lunar cycle to divine the effects of the magic, which, by then, will have been successful or failed. Divination can instruct the operator about how to adjust and adapt another working if the one that has been deployed has failed to produce the desired results.

This, then, is how to use sigils, seals, marks, signatures, and notae in magical workings. Each type of artifact has its own methodology and its own type or model of magic. Some artifacts can also be used in magical workings or used by themselves. May you use this knowledge of the notary art of magic's versatility to make your magical workings more effective and successful.

CONCLUSION

PULLING IT ALL TOGETHER: LANGUAGE AND THE NOTARY ART OF MAGIC

THE NOTARY ART, AS I HAVE DEFINED IT in this book, is a system and technology of magic that is used in nearly every single type of magical working in the Western Mystery Tradition of magic. I have never seen any system of magic where the notary art isn't used in some manner, and the fact that it can be used alone, without any other magical technology, characterizes a discipline of magic that is comprehensive and complete.

Mastering the notary art of magic is a requirement and prerequisite for mastering any other magical technology. However, I believe that I am the first magical practitioner to use this term to label a large array of different practices and associate them with a common practical philosophy: the information model of magic.

As far as I am aware, the term notary art to describe this system has not been in common use since the Renaissance, but it is a wonderful term to group this kind of magic all under one discipline. This is why *The Magical Notary Art* is an important contribution to the collection of books that separately examine these diverse methodologies. It was my design to pull them together and discuss them as variations of a single multifaceted magical discipline. I believe that grouping them together and connecting them with the information model of magic will give them greater utility and understanding as a combined set of practices.

A common thread to the notary art is that it is based on language and numbers, which are the fundamental tools for humanity seeking to understand each other and the world at large. The material and mental worlds can be given greater meaning when organized, structured, and given an ordered attribution. Numbers are the foundation of mathematics that can describe both the physical universe and the spiritual domain, just as the Pythagoreans believed ages ago. There is a physical geometry based on curved surfaces and derivative and integral processes, and there is a spiritual geometry that is pure geometric forms, structures, and archetypal numbers. Letters and numbers are the arbiters of the spiritual dimensions of consciousness, and language, whether linguistic or mathematical, defines and brings them into wholeness. If we wish to plumb the depths of the spiritual mysteries, then the artifice of letters and numbers, words and algorithms, and semantics and metaphysics represent the world that we must traverse and ultimately master.

What I have presented in this book represents the attributes of a linguistic approach to the notary art more than a mathematical one. Gematria and systems where numbers and letters are linked symbolize the place where language and mathematics converge, but there is an entire discipline of magical mathematics that is represented in the art of magic, although it is obscure and less known. My approach has been to enumerate the linguistic discipline of magic and emphasize the information theory approach to the information model of magic. Information theory has an entire body of mathematics behind it, but so does linguistics, and even semiotics has its own system of mathematics. I will leave these types of speculation where the number is king to those who have the facility for it, while I wait for someone to pursue this area of study and publish their work.

Meanwhile, I believe that I have at least covered the spectrum of linguistic based elements of the notary arts. These areas can be encapsulated by the following list of five categories.

1. Sigil Spirit Names, Seals, Signatures, and Marks
2. Sigils of Aspiration, Pictographs, Mantras, and Alphabets of Desire

3. Magical Alphabets and Letter Substitution
4. Magical Words of Power and Formulas
5. Magical Notaries and Iconic Notae

Each of these areas are used in the five models of magic: energy, spirit, psychological and temporal, stochastic, and information. Sigils of aspiration and notae can be used without any other accompanying methods of magic, so they would be considered purely a part of the information model of magic.

We have also discussed the methods to consecrate and charge these artifacts, and I shared my opinion that these magical symbols can only be activated after they are sacralized and empowered. Some might disagree with my opinion, but it is based on decades of magical workings where I used notary artifacts in many different magical operations, including by themselves.

The magical notary art is first and foremost a graphic art, and this requires individuals to become adept in the designing, crafting, and producing the artifacts that are required in many different and diverse magical operations. You must become proficient using the protractor, the compass, pen and ink, pencils, squares and triangles, Magic Markers, and many surface types, such as parchment, tag board, plywood, and metal discs and badges. There is an esthetic sensibility in this discipline that promotes an ability to draw, paint, and draft. These are skills that came naturally to me, having a talent for art and music since I was a child, but it is important for someone to learn to use these tools to produce the highest quality notary artifacts that they can accomplish. While it is acceptable to have an expert jeweler craft magical jewelry, I think that it is more important to execute notary artifacts by your own hand than to have someone else craft them for you.

It is desirable to delve deeper into these disciplines and learn to master them, so that they can be an easily crafted part of your magic. You will need to not only build them using many artistic tools, but you will need to become accomplished at visualizing and designing magical symbols and turning them into a graphical and artistic representations that will enhance the magical workings that you are seeking to perform. All of these skills take time and practice to develop, and your first attempts will be crude and not very pretty unless you can tap some inherent artistic talents or have a knack for using tools to build and craft magical devices. Some of my personal notary artifacts are quite beautiful, and others are somewhat cruder. However, I constructed these artifacts using the skills I had, and once charged and empowered, it ultimately wasn't too important as long as they worked. I have, over time, strived to be better at drawing, inking, and painting so the product of my work is appealing to me and others.

Finally, it is important to know that this magical discipline, once mastered enough to produce artifacts that are usable (and even look nice), pays dividends in how it enhances and greatly empowers all your magical operations. Since the notary art is the key to all successful magic, then learning to produce good artifacts will doubtlessly improve the level of success that you will experience when employing magic to change and improve your life materially, mentally, and spiritually.

The secret to an existence charmed by magic is to know how to build magical notary artifacts and deploy them in your magic. It is my earnest hope that I have helped you to realize this truth and set you on the path to mastering this most important magical discipline. If you were forced to master only one of the many disciplines in the art of magic, then the notary art is what you should fully master. Omitting it to study everything else would make your quest to master the art of magic a fool's errand indeed.

May the Goddesses and Gods aid you in your quest to mastery the magical notary art, and may you discover the wealth of wisdom and power that this mastery shall unlock for you.

Frater Barrabas

BIBLIOGRAPHY

Crowley, Aleister. *777 and other Qabalistic Writings of Aleister Crowley.* Samuel Weiser Inc, 1994.
Frater Barrabbas. *Mastering the Art of Witchcraft.* Crossed Crow Books, 2024.
—. *Sacramental Theurgy for Witches.* Crossed Crow Books, 2024.
—. *Talismanic Magic for Witches.* Llewellyn Publications, 2023.
—. *Elemental Power for Witches.* Llewellyn Publications, 2021.
—. *Spirit Conjuring for Witches.* Llewellyn Publications, 2017.
—. *Magical Qabalah for Beginners.* Llewellyn Publications, 2013.
Frater U. D. *Practical Sigil Magic.* Llewellyn Publications, 1990.
Huson, Paul. *Mastering Witchcraft: A Practical Guide for Witches, Warlocks, and Covens.* G. P. Putnam and Sons, 1970.
Mathers, S. L. MacGregor. *The Grimoire of Armadel.* Edited by Francis King. Samuel Weiser Inc, 1980.
Peterson, Joseph H. *The Lesser Key of Solomon.* Samuel Weiser Inc, 2001.
—. *Arbatel: Concerning the Magic of the Ancients.* Ibis Press, 2009.
Regardie, Israel. *The Golden Dawn 7th Edition.* Edited by John Michael Greer. Llewellyn Publications, 2016.
Shadrach, Nineveh. *The Occult Encyclopedia of Magic Squares.* Ishtar Publishing, 2009.
Skinner, Stephen and David Rankine. *Goetia of Dr. Rudd (Sourceworks of Ceremonial Magic).* Llewellyn Publications, 2010.

Skinner, Stephen. *Ars Noteria: The Method Version: B Mediaeval Angel Magic.* Golden Hoard Press Pte Ltd, 2021.

Stratton-Kent, Jake. *The True Grimoire: The Encyclopedia Goetica Volume 1.* Scarlet Imprint Limited, 2009.

Tyson, Donald, editor. *Three Books of Occult Philosophy written by Henry Cornelius Agrippa of Nettesheim.* Llewellyn Publications, 1997.

INDEX

A
Abramelin, 3, 18
Agrippa, 2, 5, 18, 25–26, 39
AIQ BKR, 22, 26–27, 84
Alphabet of Desire, 66, 75–76, 148
Alphabet Wheel, 3–4, 13, 28–35, 37, 53, 60
Angel, 2–3, 6, 18–19, 24, 28, 45, 48–49, 51, 61–62, 89–90, 93, 96, 112, 123–124, 142
Arbatel, 47
Ars Notoria, 2, 5, 12, 78, 89, 96
Aspiration, 1, 4, 12–14, 53–54, 63, 65–70, 76–79, 94, 120, 139, 141, 143–144, 146, 148–152, 154–155
Azazel, 51, 54–55

C
Chant, 73–74, 113, 150
Consecration, 10, 12, 33, 36, 45, 50, 52, 81, 97, 99–100, 102–103, 106, 115, 127, 129, 138, 149, 155
Crowley, Aleister, 22, 26, 60, 84

D
Dee, John, 5, 34
Deity, 2, 6–7, 11, 57, 61, 78–83, 100–101, 104–107, 115, 123–124, 126, 129, 146–149
Demon, 34, 38, 40–41, 43–45, 48–49, 53–54, 57, 61–62, 93, 112, 123–124, 142

E
Elemental, 9, 19, 117, 119, 125–126, 135, 139, 141, 144
Energy Model of Magic, 10, 66, 73, 111, 117, 119–120, 127, 138–141, 143–144, 148
Enochian, 5, 34, 75, 80, 93, 134

F
Formula, 13, 66, 82–88, 138, 155

Frater Barrabbas, 12, 103, 137, 139, 141, 143, 145, 147
Frater U.D., 66, 71, 73, 75–76, 78

G
Gematria, 20, 22, 26, 83–84, 154
Godhead, 85–86, 100–101, 103, 106, 120, 125, 129–130, 132, 134, 138, 147
Goetia, 13, 34–35, 38–41, 43–45, 48, 57
Golden Dawn, 3, 28–29, 85, 88
Greek Magical Papyri (PGM), 5, 93, 142

H
Ha-Shem, 45, 48–49

I
Icon, 93–94, 96
Information Model of Magic, 7–9, 107, 111, 119–120, 126–127, 134, 136–138, 140–141, 148, 153–155

K
Kamea, 3, 12, 17–18
Key of Solomon, 2, 39–40, 48

L
Lemegeton, 13, 39, 41
Link, 4, 8–10, 13–14, 17, 33, 36, 56, 66, 73, 78, 120, 126, 129, 135, 139–141, 143–146, 148–149
Lucifuge, 55

M
Magic Square, 3, 17–20, 24–26, 31
Magical Alphabet, 4–5, 12–13, 66, 78–82, 93–94, 138, 146, 155
Mantra, 13, 73, 75, 78, 113–114, 150, 154
Mathers, S. L. MacGregor, 45–46

N
Shadrach, Nineveh, 18–19, 26
Nota, 2, 6, 9–10, 12–14, 78, 89–97, 99–100, 102–103, 106–107, 109, 112, 115, 138, 148–152, 155
Notariqon, 20, 26, 83–84

O
Occult Philosophy, 2, 18, 25–26, 80, 83

P
Picatrix, 5
Pictogram, 1, 4, 66, 71–73, 78
Placeholder, 106, 112, 146

Q
Qabalah, 19–20, 22, 27, 84, 120, 125

S
Sacrament, 10, 100–106, 116, 126, 128, 132
Saturn, 19–20, 22–24, 51, 54, 134
Solomon, 2, 5, 39–40, 48, 89

Spare, Austin, 4, 12–13, 65–66, 71, 73, 75–76, 78
Spirit Model of Magic, 10, 111, 123, 140, 142

T

Talisman, 5, 14, 18, 31, 102, 106, 124, 128, 135–136, 144–146, 148
Talismanic, 19, 91, 107, 117, 123, 134–137, 144–148
Tarot, 56–61, 115
Temurah, 20, 22, 26–27, 83–84
Theban Alphabet, 80
Theurgy, 103, 107, 146–147, 151
Tyson, Donald, 25–26, 80

V

Vasago, 4, 35
Verba Ignota, 6, 89

W

Weyer, Johann, 39
Word of Power, 1–3, 5–7, 13, 66, 73–75, 79–83, 87, 89, 92–94, 114, 150, 155

Z

Zazel, 22, 24, 27